What's Next?
Professional Development
Advice

From php[architect] Magazine

Edited By
Oscar Merida

 a php[architect] anthology

What's Next? Professional Development Advice

First Edition: February 2017
ISBN - print: 978-1-940111-51-3
ISBN - PDF: 978-1-940111-52-0
ISBN - epub: 978-1-940111-53-7
ISBN - mobi: 978-1-940111-54-4
ISBN - safari: 978-1-940111-55-1
Produced & Printed in the United States

Contributors

Published by
musketeers.me, LLC.
201 Adams Ave.
Alexandria, VA 22301 USA

240-348-5PHP (240-348-5747)
info@phparch.com
www.phparch.com

Editor-in-Chief
Oscar Merida

Layout and Design
Kevin Bruce

Table of Contents

Contributors

Cal Evans

These days, when not working with PHP, Cal can be found working on a variety of projects like Nomad PHP. He speaks at conferences around the world on topics ranging from technical talks to motivational talks for developers . *@calevans*

Joe Devon

Joe Devon has been developing in PHP since Version 3. He is an advisor or board member at various companies, non-profits and conferences. He is Founding Partner of LAPHP user group; Diamond, a Digital Agency in Venice; Television Four, a Digital Media startup and Global Accessibility Awareness Day (#GAAD). He is passionate about Digital Accessibility & encouraging the UX & Development Community to produce accessible content. He blogs at http://dws.la/author/joedevon and may be reached on LinkedIn, http://linkedin.com/in/joedevon, Twitter @joedevon and email at phparch@dws.la.

Steve Grunwell

Steve Grunwell is a Senior Web Engineer at 10up, living and working in Columbus, OH. When he's not writing software, he can be found speaking at conferences, blogging about software development, or continuing his search for the perfect cup of coffee. *@stevegrunwell*

Stefan Koopmanschap

Stefan Koopmanschap runs his own business called Ingewikkeld, organizes WeCamp, and has been involved in starting several usergroups in The Netherlands and BeNeLux. *@skoop*

Ole Michaelis

Ole Michaelis is the co-founder of SoCoded, a hackfest and web development conference in Hamburg. He is a Software Engineer at Jimdo, a DIY website creator, where he focuses on backend development. In his free time, he's building slidr.io, a hassle-free slide sharing platform. Ole is passionate about open source software, enjoys traveling, and loves Mexican food. He classifies himself as a 'bad' German as he dislikes beer and soccer – the traditional German past-times. *@CodeStars*

Joshua Silver

Joshua Silver is VP, Product Development and the technical co-founder of Patientco, a healthcare IT and payments startup in Atlanta. At Patientco, he is responsible for overall product direction, R&D initiatives, and technology strategy. Joshua has over a decade of development (mostly PHP/MySQL) and product management experience and frequently speaks on topics such as consumer-centric system design, secure payment processing, and scalable web architecture. Joshua holds a BS in Computer Science from GA Tech. When not working, Joshua is most likely traveling and has been to nearly 30 countries.

Gabriel Somoza

Gabriel Somoza is a Belgium-based PHP architect with a strong background in Ecommerce. He spends most of his time consulting through Strategery—his development boutique specializing in building highly-customized web applications and e-commerce stores. He's also a *ZCE* and *Magento Certified Developer (Plus)*. He is active in the open-source community with contributions to Doctrine Migrations, ZF2, and is the author of the Strategery InfiniteScroll extension for Magento. He's the organizer of PHP Limburg, a meetup with 120+ registered members in Belgium. When not working, he spends time with his beautiful wife, travels, and researches new ways of applying technology to solve old problems. *@gabriel_somoza*

David Stockton

David Stockton is a husband, father and Software Developer. He builds software in Colorado, leading a few teams of software developers creating a very diverse array of web applications. His two daughters, age 11 and 9, are learning to code JavaScript, Python, Scratch, a bit of Java and PHP as well as building electrical circuits, and a 4 year old son who has been seen studying calculus, equating monads to monoids in the category of endofunctors, and is excelling at annoying his sisters. David is a conference speaker and an active proponent of TDD, APIs and elegant PHP. He's on twitter as *@dstockto* and can be reached by email at *levelingup@davidstockton.com*.

Jordan Tway

Jordan Tway is a lead recruiter at Robert Half Technology. In his free time, he loves to stay active! That includes lifting weights, playing basketball, soccer, sand volleyball, golf, flag football, and he is currently training for the Ironman 70.3 Triathlon in Racine. On Wisconsin and Go Pack Go! Outside of staying active, he likes to meet new people, listen to music, hang with friends in the area, and relax. Before Robert Half, he was enrolled at the University of Wisconsin-Whitewater studying Marketing with an emphasis in Direct and Internet Marketing. He always enjoys connecting with people so feel free to look him up on LinkedIn or follow him on Twitter! *@JTway23*

Joshua Warren

Joshua Warren has been developing with PHP since 1999. He is the Founder of Creatuity, where he works on eCommerce projects with Magento and Yii. He founded Creatuity in 2008 as a development agency and has grown it to a team of over 25 including 14 developers working across 2 continents. When Joshua isn't developing, he enjoys traveling to new countries to try local food and beer while meeting developers at local meetups. You can follow him on Twitter or on his blog http://joshuawarren.com

Eli White

Eli White is the Conference Chair for php[architect] and Vice President of One for All Events, LLC. He has a BS in CS, but it was so long ago he probably doesn't remember any of it at this point. *@EliW*

Trip Witt

Trip Witt is a web application developer with ten years experience living in Lynchburg, Virginia. He works for Advanced Manufacturing Technology, Inc. creating and maintaining information systems and custom web applications both internal and client-specific. When he was just 27 he was named one of Central Virginia's Top Movers and Shakers for his website development with the American Red Cross. Customer focused and driven to exceed expectations, he is always wanting to learn more and thrives to develop new applications to make life easier for the end user. *@trip_witt*

Chapter

1

Professional Development for Professional Developers

Steve Grunwell

Programming is often a full-time job, but so is being a part of the programming community. With new technologies, tools, and buzzwords popping up every week, how can a professional stay on top of his or her game without going completely insane?

As developers, we have one of the best jobs in the world: we get to solve problems every day, reducing "real" business problems into puzzles made of data, logic, and code. Rather than performing hard, backbreaking labor, we have the luxury of being presented with a situation and tasked with instructing a machine how best to handle it.

We developers are artisans: Our studio, an office or coffee shop; our tool, a keyboard; our canvas: a text editor. As such, we mustn't rest on our laurels but strive to be better, constantly growing and improving. With so much to see and do, how can a programmer—especially one with a full-time career—continue to hone his or her craft?

The following guidelines come from nearly a decade of software development experience—a self-study driven by passion, curiosity, and taking tremendous pride in a job well done. Whether you're a computer science student, a self-taught developer just getting started, or a seasoned professional, these nuggets of wisdom can help you be the developer you've always wanted to be.

Programming Should be Your Passion

Whether a fresh-faced junior or a battle-tested senior, the best trait you can possess as a developer is to be passionate about what you do. You don't have to dream in code (though it probably doesn't hurt), but 4 out of 5 dentists agree that someone passionate about their work has infinitely more potential than someone who is talented but lacks ambition.

What does it mean to be passionate? It means finding yourself thinking about the best way to tackle a problem, even when you're off the clock. Being so excited to try out a new framework or technique that you look up at the clock and realize it's past midnight. Passion is that euphoric release you get when you've finally shipped your code and you feel as though **there's no problem you can't solve.**

I'll caution you, however, to not confuse a passion for an obsession. Being a great developer does not mean chaining your life to the keyboard, churning out code until your eyes bleed. The best developers know the value of engaging in activities away from the computer (you know, the "real" world), and the best employers will recognize this, too.

I don't play the lottery, but when the jackpots get high people love to talk about what they'd do were they to strike it rich. When people ask me what *I* would do, I always give the same answer: "If money were no object and I didn't have to work, I'd still be writing software, **but it would be the software I want to write.**"

Sure, I'd probably have a beach house somewhere, and I might be too busy traveling the world to put in a regular 40-hour work week, but software will always be a part of my life *because* it's something that I'm passionate about.

Keep Up with the Industry...

...but not *everything* going on. The software industry is constantly changing, and it can be a struggle to keep up with news about the technologies you're *already* using, never mind the new frameworks, libraries, and workflows that are popping up every week.

Relax, no (reasonable) person is expecting you to be the expert on everything. Once you accept this fact, the fear and anxiety around keeping up with *all the things!* should fade away.

Find the ways to get news that fit your lifestyle the best, be it Twitter, RSS feeds, magazines, or user groups. Look up profiles of other professionals you admire, and see who *they* are following. Seek out Slack channels relevant to your interests, and subscribe to newsletters that compile the news of the day or the week for you.

Attend a conference (or several). Sit in on a session about a new technology you've been curious about but haven't had time to research; even half an hour of hearing firsthand experiences about a tool can be far more beneficial than hours of grokking documentation and "Hello World" apps.

If you don't have the time or budget for a conference (or you don't like to travel), seek out remote learning opportunities like NomadPHP[1]. Most larger cities have locally organized monthly meetups, too.

The world of software development moves pretty fast; if you don't stop and look around once in a while, you could miss it.

Don't Worry About What Other People are Doing

It's not a new phenomenon, but our hyperconnected world only amplifies the "Fear of Missing Out" (FOMO). Everyone's talking about #phpcruise on Twitter, but you have a scheduling conflict. Your coworker is flying across the world to give a keynote at a conference, and you're just binge-watching shows on Netflix.

It's easy to look at the fun that other people are having and feel as though you're missing out, but what we often fail to realize is that we're comparing the entirety of our lives to someone else's highlight reel. Are you really "slacking off" in the community, or are you choosing to spend your evenings with your family instead? Don't let a single interest, no matter how passionate you are, consume you.

One thing that unifies every person on Earth, rich or poor, is that we only have so many hours in a day; balance them among your passions and interests, let others do the same, and share your experiences together. You're not missing out, you're simply spending your time differently.

Keep an Eye on Your Stress Levels

Writing software isn't always a walk in the park, and it's very easy to fall prey to taking on too much work in too little time. Perhaps it was a bad estimate and now you're in over your head, or maybe your sales team committed to an unrealistic timeline, but we've all faced times where we felt under the gun to deliver.

Relax. Take a deep breath. Very few of us are writing code that would cause irreparable harm if it didn't work perfectly (this advice does not apply, however, to those programming weapons targeting systems, automated transportation, and/or medical equipment), so don't treat every deadline like a life-or-death situation. If it seems like you might not be able to fully deliver on time, work with your team and the project stakeholders to adjust expectations; you may be surprised how understanding people can be.

If your employer offers you paid vacation time, take advantage of it (and if they don't, find an employer who does); burnout is a **very** real thing, and if you're not careful you may find yourself loathing this career which, as we've already established, you should be passionate about. Even the best of us know that sometimes it's necessary to unplug for a while and recharge our mental

[1] NomadPHP: https://nomadphp.com

batteries. Take a trip, pick up a new hobby, or enjoy the timeless tradition of the "staycation" and veg out on the couch.

If the burnout doesn't recede, find someone you trust to talk to about how you're feeling. There's a frightening number of developers living with mental health issues, including depression and anxiety. Fortunately, there are also organizations dedicated to providing support for those in the technology industry suffering from these illnesses. Learn about mental health and its treatments, find out what mental health benefits your employer offers, and know that **there's no shame in seeking help**. Some community resources to check out include:

- Prompt: Mental Health in the Technology Industry—_http://mhprompt.org_
- Open Sourcing Mental Illness—_http://funkatron.com/osmi_
- Mental Health First Aid—_http://www.mentalhealthfirstaid.org_

Keep a Record of Your Ideas

When your mind is geared to solve problems, you can never be sure when inspiration might strike. Find a way to write down these ideas to revisit later; I've found that Evernote[2] can be great for this, as my ideas are synchronized between my computer and phone. I also keep pens and pads of paper around the house and in my car, just in case something hits me when I'm away from a screen.

Make a point of periodically going back through these ideas. Some will be laughable or completely off-the-wall, but you might surprise yourself with what you dream up when you're not actively _trying_ to invent something.

Having a place to keep track of ideas for later can also be a great way to stay focused on the task at hand and not get distracted; sometimes a client call or a watercooler chat with a coworker is enough to spark an idea, but you if you can't afford to spend the time fully exploring it (or don't want to risk doing that on company time), jot down as much as you can and keep the note handy throughout the day. As it stews on your mental back burner, add details to the note as they form, so you don't miss anything when you revisit the idea at a later date.

Open-Source FTW

The barrier to entry for developers has never been lower, and that's due largely in part to open-source software. These tools, open to examine and often free to use, make the cost of getting started with software development almost nil (you still need a computer and an Internet connection, after all).

Need an editor? Atom is free and gaining lots of attention. An operating system? There are dozens of flavors of Linux, free for you to install and modify to your heart's content. An astonishing amount of the Web runs entirely on open-source software, and many of its authors welcome outside contributions.

[2] Evernote, free: _https://evernote.com_

Do you wish that program could do X? Awesome, reach out to the authors and suggest it. If you're able, write the feature yourself and open a pull request; your dream feature could become a permanent part of the application for everyone to use, and before long the original author may be asking for *your* advice on how the project should move forward!

Open-source software can also be a tremendous educational tool; instead of treating our software as mysterious black boxes, free and open-source software (FOSS) pops the hood and lets you see how the internals work together. When you're learning a new language or framework, there's nothing better than being able to poke around the codebase of a real, in-the-wild application.

Employers love open-source, too: there's no better way to prove "I know how the internals of this software work" than being listed as a project contributor. If you're in the market for a new job—especially if you're just breaking into programming—making open-source contributions is one of the single best things you can do to bolster your résumé, attract recruiters, and break into the software community.

Code Speaks Louder than Words

You can read every blog, complete every tutorial, and spend hours a day working on Code Katas, but the ultimate test of your knowledge is shipping working production code. At some point, every developer must finally commit (no pun intended) to pushing code out to the world.

Yeah, it's scary. Maybe you made some mistakes. What if they don't like it? What if they told you you're no good? Well buck up, George McFly, because making mistakes and getting feedback is how we better ourselves.

Put that pet project up on GitHub and tweet out a link. Ask your colleagues, mentors, and other trusted professionals to take it for a spin. With any luck, someone will find a bug or some weird edge case you hadn't considered. The next time you look at this problem, you'll remember that and approach it differently.

Likewise, if you're using an open-source tool and find a bug, don't be afraid to let the author know. These works are often labors of love, and if you're having a problem with it there's a good chance you're not the only one. Offer to help the author fix the issue, even if just by way of a good bug report. It's easy to be an armchair programmer, proclaiming "that software sucks"; put your money where your mouth is and write something awesome.

Never Stop Learning

The day a programmer decides that he or she have learned everything they need to know is the day that coder's professional development comes to a screeching halt. There are *always* new things to learn, new ideas to be explored, and old assumptions to be questioned.

Make sure you're regularly revisiting old projects, even if you're not responsible for maintaining them. Is that code something you'd ship today? If the answer is "no" (or "not without some refactoring") then congratulations, you're a better developer than you were when you wrote that code months ago!

> *If you don't find at least one thing that makes you cringe in code you wrote six months ago, you might be doing it wrong.*

The new things you choose to study don't even have to be directly related to your area of expertise. Moving at your own pace, learn Ruby on Rails and see how you can apply its principles to your next PHP app. Write something in Python just to try it out. Dig into the internals of a library you use all the time to figure out how it works, what makes it tick. These are all activities that will broaden your horizons to what other languages, frameworks, and communities are doing. Then, take that knowledge back to your own work and repeat the cycle.

Find (and be) a Mentor

Mentorship is one of the single best ways for someone to get stronger in an area of study. Whether a formal, scheduled mentorship or an ad hoc relationship with someone you can bounce ideas off of, a mentor helps you grow, challenges your assumptions, and shares the benefit of his or her experiences.

My first mentor, Matt, was a web designer at work. At the time, I was doing mostly video production until my boss asked if I could try to make heads or tails out of some PHP a former employee had written. With only some BASIC programming under my belt, I started deconstructing the code, figuring out how it all worked. Whenever I'd get stumped, I'd pop into Matt's office and ask him if he could explain it to me.

Before long, I got the hang of writing PHP applications. Matt and I would toss ideas around during lunch, and I'd try to build them in the evening. Naturally, there were a lot of projects that never got off the ground and the code was primitive, but these exercises gave me the confidence that so many junior developers sorely lack.

I've had many more mentors throughout my career, but it's only recently that I've embraced the idea of acting as a formal mentor for other developers. If you have experiences to share, I'd encourage you not only to learn from mentors but to pay that favor forward by joining an organization like PHP Mentoring[3].

Learn About Humility

Programmers tend to be logical, analytical people; we don't run from a problem, but instead try to reason out the best way to approach it. Even if our grades didn't necessarily reflect it, I'd be willing to bet a fair number of us would say that school came "pretty easily" to us, forcing us

---

[3]   *PHP Mentoring:* https://phpmentoring.org

to satisfy that urge for mental stimulation through advanced coursework, extracurriculars, or tinkering (whether the faculty approved or not).

Being one of the smartest people in the room throughout school can make for a rude awakening when you start your career. Even if you're an A-player within your company, you're bound to cross paths with someone in the community who knows more than you do.

When this happens, there are a few ways to handle it: you could feel threatened, become confrontational, get exiled from the community, and live with a chip on your shoulder forever, **or** you could admit that this person may know more about this one specific topic, learn from him or her, and then share what you've learned with the larger community. The choice is yours, but only one lets you…

Be a Positive Force in Your Community

Believe it or not, computers don't care what race, gender, sexual orientation, religion, or age their programmers are. There's nothing that makes a 27-year-old white male a better programmer than a 55-year-old Latina woman, yet some bad apples in the development community seem to think it's okay to proclaim otherwise. These people are known as "trolls," and **we do not feed the trolls!**

If you don't fit into the stereotypical model of "a programmer," **good!** The technology industry isn't meant to be some exclusive club where you need to know the secret handshake to be accepted. Rather than dividing ourselves, we should celebrate the different viewpoints that a rich, diverse community can offer. You can do your part by being open to new ideas, accepting of all well-intentioned community members, and not being afraid to call someone out when they're making other people feel threatened or unwelcome.

We're All in This Together

No two developers are exactly alike, nor will their journeys be exactly the same. Take comfort in knowing that you're a part of the larger software community, a fraternity of creative thinkers, problem-solvers, tinkerers, and puzzlers. Our industry is one where a little curiosity can open entirely new worlds, so ask questions, try new things, and never stop moving forward.

Chapter 2

More Than Just an "OK" Dev

Gabriel Somoza

In today's web development market there are tons of job openings with excellent salaries and perks like cars, work-from-home arrangements, unlimited holidays, opportunities to become certified, and so on. But how long until the bubble bursts? A growing number of people are being raised to become programmers, and some have been programming since before they could even talk. Are you ready to compete with the upcoming waves of younger, smarter developers?

I was raised in Argentina, one of a few countries where you wouldn't necessarily be surprised to learn that your taxi driver had a medical degree. As in many other parts of the world, doctors in Argentina are overworked and underpaid.

At the other end of the spectrum, we developers experience almost the exact opposite. Companies are competing very aggressively to attract talent, to the point of basically treating developers like rockstars—giving them beautiful company cars, unlimited holidays, remote work arrangements, and even four-day work weeks, all on top of an average U.S. salary of nearly six figures—and well above that in some other places.

When considering the contrasting working conditions of these two professions, one thing is clear: we're living in the golden age of web development. In the words of Silicon Valley developer James Somers[1]: "In this particular gold rush (of tech startups) the shovel is me."

Such market conditions can foster developer complacency and professional stagnation. For example, a developer might stay long-term at a comfortable and well-paid job that's not challenging enough for his or her career, and could simply lose the drive to learn new things.

I regularly hire developers and frequently encounter applicants who seem content to stagnate. As I interviewed people, I learned to quickly identify certain characteristics that, in most cases, make all the difference between someone being an "OK" developer and an outstanding one. I have listed some of them below, along with some advice on how to build them into your career toolbox.

1. Engages with the Community

This refers to developers who regularly attend meetups or conferences and, usually, are active on IRC, Slack, and other online forums.

Ideally, the developer is a community **enabler**: actively helps organize events, regularly speaks at meetups or conferences, and provides support in online technical communities. A community enabler can communicate and solve complex interpersonal problems beyond the realm of code.

These traits are valuable because communities are bigger than individuals. A developer actively involved in the community is connected to something larger than himself and will therefore have continual access to:

1. New ideas, which can prevent stagnation.
2. Other experts and specialists, including the problem-solving resources and potential new hires they can supply. Such value is often overlooked.
3. Mentors.

Starting to Participate in the Community

The development community will gladly help you to integrate if you show interest. You can start by joining a local meetup (try *http://meetup.com*). Twitter, IRC, and Slack are great venues when you're having trouble or if you're willing to grow by helping others.

2. Contributes to Open Source

Open source is the heart of PHP, and I've come to realize that great PHP developers understand this. Contributing to Open Source projects is therefore one of the best ways to give back to the community.

I now rarely consider hiring someone for a senior position if that person doesn't have publicly

[1]   *Web Developer: It's A Little Insane How Well-Paid And In-Demand I AM: http://phpa.me/bi-webdev-demand*

available contributions, even just a personal project. The project must be complete, and, ideally, it should be a reusable library that solves a well-defined problem.

When reviewing a developer's public code, it's important to look for the basic indicators of a good developer: automated tests, a well-defined coding style, documentation, design, license inclusion, proper use of patterns, proper use of Composer (including a good choice of dependencies), and so forth.

A developer who regularly contributes to open source displays the following characteristics:

1. experience designing code for reusability
2. self-motivation and proactivity
3. attention to detail

Other ways of giving back to the community, such as mentoring, will be discussed later in this article .

Starting to Contribute to Open Source

When I wanted to start contributing, many people told me that I simply had to submit a pull request. My problem was not knowing *what* to contribute. Eventually, I realized that getting started is not so much about chasing a great idea as it is about coding with a specific *mindset* of solidarity: "Will this code I'm writing be valuable to the community?" The answer is probably **yes** if you:

1. Fixed a bug
2. Found a better way of doing things (something faster, less resource-intensive, more flexible, etc.)
3. Found something that your framework was missing. For example, one of my first pull requests was a Whitelist and Blacklist filter for Zend Framework 2.
4. Created something modular that can be reused with a framework, or even by itself.
5. Helped to document a framework or library
6. Added automated tests for a framework or library

As you explore the mindset and become familiar with the above, you'll find many other opportunities to contribute code, and ultimately give back to the community.

TIP #1: *Before spending a lot of time working on a new feature or fixing a bug on a project, go to the project's issue tracker and make sure there are no open issues related to that.*

TIP #2: *If you're contributing a new feature or a backwards-incompatible change, make sure you open a new ticket on the project's issue tracker to discuss it first, before you spend time working on it. The project maintainer may have different plans in mind, so first make sure your efforts will be well received!*

3. Learns from Mentors

> *A mentor is a person or friend who guides a less experienced person by building trust and modeling positive behaviors. An effective mentor understands that his or her role is to be dependable, engaged, authentic, and tuned into the needs of the mentee[2].*

It's relatively common for people to find a mentor because it's natural for human beings to transmit knowledge from generation to generation. Many people have one (or more) mentors during their careers without even realizing it: a teacher at school, a family member, a colleague or boss, or even a consultant working at their company.

When I look back I realize my career wouldn't be the same if it wasn't for the mentors I had.

For me, it started early: when I was around 11 years old my computer teacher saw that I had an interest in programming. While most other kids were learning how to type without looking at the keyboard, he would invest time to show me how to build a few things in Macromedia Flash 5 (ActionScript). That's how I started to build my first Flash games and websites, and how I developed the passion for web development that I still have today. Since then I've been lucky to always have at least one mentor in my life. Eventually it became a conscious choice: I started to actively look for mentors to coach me on several aspects of my career.

One of the main reasons I search for developers who have mentors is that I know I'll be hiring someone who has direct access to a pool of knowledge and experience that's larger than the individual. This is similar to the concept of being tapped into a community, except that in this case it carries the stronger bond of a deeper relationship.

Finding a Mentor

There are many paths to finding a good mentor, but in my experience the best mentoring relationships happen **organically**. The most important ingredients that help these organic relationships to develop are being involved in the community and giving back to it—which, not by coincidence, are the first two items discussed in this list. While doing that you'll cross paths with people that you'll start to admire.

Once you find the right person, the next step is formalizing the relationship. There are many articles online on how to engage with a potential mentor and ultimately define and formalize the relationship.

Last but not least, in the PHP community there's a project at *http://php-mentoring.org* specifically designed to help people find mentors. The site also has more information about the benefits of mentoring as well as a directory of people who are willing to mentor. I encourage you to check it out!

[2] *Module 3: What is a Mentor and Roles of the Mentor and Mentee: http://www.oycp.com/MentorTraining/3/m3.html*

Becoming a Mentor

As I developed my career I had the opportunity to mentor developers myself, and found that being a mentor is an excellent way to learn even more. In other words, it's a two-way street for both the mentor and the mentee.

Becoming a mentor is a bit more difficult than finding one. though, because you have to be approached, which requires a certain level of recognition and respect. But once again the key ingredient is community: become a community **enabler**, be ready to help, lead by example, always while being respectful of others, and you'll soon become someone's role model.

4. Is a Full-Stack Integrator

This is something I realized only recently: the value of the "full stack developer" title is getting diluted because, as technology evolves, most levels of the stack are becoming highly special-ized. It's not only hard to become a full-stack developer: it's *even harder* to maintain the requisite knowledge. It is therefore becoming increasingly rare to find someone who truly qualifies as a full-stack developer.

Instead of looking for full stack developers, I look for people who qualify as **full-stack integra-tors**. These people may specialize in an area such as back-end PHP development, but they have enough end-to-end architectural skills to integrate new technologies fairly easily, even without extensive knowledge. For example, they may be able to quickly build an API to communicate with an Ember.js front end, even without having worked with Ember.js before. They may even be able to change existing Ember.js code without spending much time reading documentation.

Some key characteristics of full-stack integrators:

1. They can filter noise. This allows them to skim documentation very quickly and extract only the information they really need to solve the problem at hand.
2. They have 90/10 skills, meaning that they're skilled with one specific technology (the 90 part), but they also have basic skills and experience in a wide range of other technologies across most levels of a modern web stack.
3. I've found that these people usually market themselves as specialists, not as full-stack developers. However, their job applications and public code make them stand out from pure specialists by showing that they're not afraid to get their hands dirty with new technologies.
4. They share a deep passion for technology and rarely say things like "technology X is the best"; they know when to apply the right technology.
5. Many of them are either leading development teams or running their own companies, which allows them to practice their skills as needed.

Becoming a Full-Stack Integrator

Becoming a full-stack integrator requires many years of experience integrating, designing, and delivering solutions with different technologies. Most of the people I've worked with who have this experience have pivoted their web stack at least once (usually multiple times) during their careers. For example, they went from being a senior Rails or Java developer to a NodeJS developer, then moved to PHP.

Becoming a full-stack integrator is also supported by a shift in paradigms: OOP to functional, monolithic to micro-services, CRUD to DDD, etc. This provides deep architectural understanding, which is essential for successfully designing and integrating an application's technology stack.

5. Follows Coding Standards and Best Practices

A typical code review involves looking at the cleanliness of the code, the extent to which it's documented, the presence of tests, and so on. Looking under the hood, many of these indicators are related to how much a developer respects code—not only her own but also that of others—to the extent that she will follow a set of coding standards and best practices.

Coding standards offer several benefits to adopters: sustainability, interoperability, reduced cognitive overhead, reduced risk, improved productivity, and more. Some have become so widely adopted in the PHP community that they're indispensable for modern web development: a clear example is PSR-4 (the Autoloader standard). They therefore reflect some of the things that the community, company, or project behind them finds important—such as the need for better interoperability between frameworks in the case of the standards recommended by the PHP-FIG[3]. Although adhering to them can be beneficial at a project level, it is ultimately also a way of showing empathy and respect to the community that recommends them.

When hiring senior PHP developers I consider adherence to major standards and best practices a strict "must" (except when properly justified). I've found they can work as great filters during interviews: if the person can't tell me what the first 4 PSRs are about without googling it, then they're immediately discarded from the process. The same thing happens if their open source code doesn't follow a clear coding standard.

All great PHP developers I know of follow coding standards (such as PSRs or PEAR) and best practices (such as writing automated tests). And if they don't follow one of them, they usually **document** an excellent reason why, providing useful information for future developers in the project.

Learning About the Latest Standards and Best Practices

My favorite go-to resource for learning about the latest PHP development standards and best practices is the PHP The Right Way website[4]. If you haven't visited it yet I strongly encourage you to do so—the site includes many other resources and links (mostly technical) that will help you become a better developer.

If you already know about these standards and best practices but you feel you don't have a

[3] PHP-FIG: http://www.php-fig.org
[4] PHP The Right Way website: http://www.phptherightway.com

deep grasp of the subject yet, the best way to cement your knowledge is to apply it. Next time you work on a project, for example, make sure it has the following elements:

1. A `CONTRIBUTING.md` file (or equivalent) that explains in detail which standards the project adheres to.
2. A test suite that includes static code analysis to enforce those standards. You can use CodeSniffer[5] and PHP Mess Detector[6] to help you with that.
3. A build tool to automate those tests, such as Phing[7] or Ant[8].

> **TIP:** *You can contribute a pull-request to any open-source package that doesn't do this yet, as a way of giving back to the community!*

I find there have been few things more satisfying in my career than the opportunities I've had to learn technologies and get involved with the communities around them; and there's been nothing more inspiring than following the example of those ahead of me. Discovering the value of community has also refueled my passion for web development in moments when it was dwindling, and I know it has the potential to do so for many years to come.

Conclusion

To conclude, we briefly examined some characteristics that can help you stand out beyond your code. Even better: they will help you stand out *within the community*—with all of the benefits and responsibility that entails. As you might have realized, we barely scratched the surface on each of them—and there are many more—so I encourage you to pick one, start to develop it today, and learn more as you go!

[5] *CodeSniffer: https://github.com/squizlabs/PHP_CodeSniffer*
[6] *PHP Mess Detector: https://phpmd.org*
[7] *Phing: https://www.phing.info*
[8] *Ant: http://ant.apache.org*

Chapter

3

How to Burn the Candle at Both Ends

David Stockton

If you're a professional developer—and chances are, since you're reading this article, you are—you've likely been given a deadline that felt unreasonable or a task that felt insurmountable, or a project that seemed like it was set up to fail from the start. I don't think I've met any developer who hasn't had this happen. If this doesn't describe you, I'd like to meet you and learn about your place of employment.

For many developers, dealing with poor projects and bad project managers is an unfortunate reality. They are given work to do with no input regarding what or how long it will take to get it done. Then, when it takes longer than expected, it's the fault of the developer. This is no good. Fortunately, there's a solution, but we'll get to that in a bit.

A Personal Story

When I was interviewed for my current position, one of the first questions I was asked was if I could—or, more likely, would—fire a particular developer on the team. Now, it just so happened that this developer happened to be the one who recommended me for the job. Fast-forward to today: those two individuals are no longer employed with us, but the developer who I was supposed to fire is still here and kicking. However, that's not the story I wanted to tell, so we'll jump back several years to my interviews.

One of the next things that happened in the interviews was that I was told by a number of different individuals, including the project manager, how much of a mess the development team was. I asked for the project manager to elaborate and tell me about what was going on.

The project manager (PM) told me the development team never got anything done on time; they were constantly late; and the software was buggy and required constant hotfixes and maintenance between scheduled releases.

I asked this individual if the developers understood what they were building and if they had an idea of the big picture. The PM told me that the the big picture was understood by the PM and that each of the developers was told the bits that the PM had determined they needed to know. Furthermore, the PM didn't have the time to explain all of this to "those d@$% developers."

Now, knowing that the developers didn't have any idea about what they were building, I asked how the time estimates were made. Did the developers assigned to each piece of work come up with estimates on their own, or did one developer come up with estimates for everyone?

I was told that neither of these were correct; in fact, the project manager came up with all of the estimates and made all of the work assignments without any input from the developers. I asked if the PM had ever developed software or done web development. I was told that "I didn't understand that s@#$."

At this point, with many of my instincts telling me to run away, I decided to see if I could learn any more. I asked if this process had worked out well so far. I was told that the developers were always late and constantly building the wrong thing (ya think?). I asked how the PM was expecting this to work considering their complete lack of experience actually building software, as well as the fact that the developers had never been consulted about what it would take to build, not to mention that they had no idea about what they were building beyond the myopic view of the software that the PM deemed worthy to share with them. Obviously, I didn't word things quite like that—it was an interview, after all.

My diagnosis on the major cause of the problem was not the same as theirs—to say the least. Clearly, there's a problem when the development team has no input in the process and has no idea what they are building or how it even fit into the big picture.

Changing the Culture

Long story slightly shorter, I still ended up taking the job. I've had an interesting career so far, ranging from jobs where I was doing way less than I was capable of to others where I was doing much more than I should be. After experiencing a wide range of cultures that I didn't feel were conducive to being a well-adjusted, productive developer, and having no real way to make any positive changes, moving into management seemed like a way I could make a difference for a lot of developers who may end up having a better start to their career than I had.

Over the last few years, we've made a number of improvements. We've moved from Subversion to Mercurial; we've move from FlySpray (a bug tracker that was on the third page of Google results when I searched for it by name) to Rally and then JIRA. We've started to move to continuous deployment/delivery, to say nothing of the continuous integration that has been occurring for years. Unit testing is the norm now, and TDD is happening more and more frequently. However, all of these things by themselves do not help with changing the attitude of a company that sees developers as replaceable cogs in a machine who turn ideas into code and code into money factories.

Only a shift in culture will help with that, and it's one that we are continuing to work on and change. Moving away from a culture that looks at the 40-hour work week as the bare minimum is not easy, but in order to get away from the death marches and the poorly planned and executed projects, it must be done. Developers have agreed to give up some of their time in exchange for a paycheck, but cultures where it is expected that developers eat, breathe, sleep, and bleed code are toxic and must be changed. If you cannot change it and you don't trust your managers to change it, for your own sake, please consider working elsewhere. There are plenty of places looking for developers that do have a healthy culture with a good balance between work and life.

Knowledge is powerful. One of the most empowering changes we were able to make was to turn work into a learning-friendly place. We encourage people to try out new techniques and technologies, as well as learn about them and how they might help make our products better and even how they may open up new opportunities for new business and new products. Some managers are worried about training their people because then the employees are more valuable and thus more likely to be snatched up or enticed by a better offer elsewhere. This is true. Employees who train and learn new things are more valuable, and some of them will leave. On the other hand, if they are not learning, they are stagnating. Perhaps it's worse that those who are stagnating don't leave.

What Was the Point?

I started out writing this article thinking that I'd write about burnout and how to recognize it and avoid it, as well as possibly how to recover from it if you find out that it's happening to you. And I will still end up talking about that. It's funny, too, as this past week I've seen quite a lot of talk on Twitter about burnout and related topics. Perhaps it's no more than usual, and I've just been more sensitive to it lately because burnout has been on my mind. I also feel like I may be one of the worst people to talk about that topic (hooray, Impostor Syndrome!). I'm most likely to tell my employees that they should not work extra time or outside of work to figure something out even if it would help a project finish sooner while simultaneously doing the opposite. Do as I say, not as I do, right?

Never, in the time I've been here, have I asked my team to work a holiday or weekend in order to get something done. That's not to say that holiday or weekend or evening work hasn't happened. But at this point, any work outside normal hours is happening without me asking for it. All this leads me to another story, hopefully one that won't get me into too much trouble, but in any case, here goes.

The Story of Face Punch Day

Going into the end of the year, 2010, we had a deadline dictated to the team (the culture was still completely broken at this time, as I'd only been on the job for a couple of months). We were going to get a new portion of one of our main products built, and we were going to get some 14,000 new clients on it by the end of the year. The end of the year happened, and the product wasn't done, so the deadline moved to February. February came and went, then April, then May. May 30th, 2011 was Memorial Day, and the entire team was required to be at work—on a holiday—to hopefully complete this project that had no chance of getting done that day. Tensions were high, but we did our time and—surprise, surprise—when we left for the day, there was still work to be done.

"Face Punch Day" was actually the following day, Tuesday morning, and a few of us had gotten in rather early to try to get a head start on this project that was really nowhere near completion. Early in the morning, a rather heated discussion happened between two rather high-level individuals (both at the executive level) regarding a decision that had been made a few months prior that apparently upset the VP. This turned into a screaming match that traveled across the length of the building, heading toward the front door and with threats including, "I'm going to punch your &@#$ing face off" being yelled.

Once the yelling died down and both individuals were sent home, the rest of the team was left with a lot of uncertainty and worry, both with what, if anything, this altercation (or near altercation) meant to their continued employment and what was to become of the individuals involved. Eventually, their fate was decided, but it was clear that a toxic environment combined with stress and ego lead to an explosion of emotions and words, as well as a display that should have been handled in a much better way. No actual punching of faces happened, but we continue to observe a day of remembrance each Tuesday after Memorial Day.

Rarely do dysfunctional teams have such a unifying event as this to make it very clear that the current path is extremely broken and must be fixed. This still took some time, but since then, I don't think there has been an instance—that I'm aware of—of our developers being required to work overtime. Many aspects of our culture have improved drastically since then, but in many ways, both culturally and technologically, we're still quite a ways from where I'd like us to be.

Where We Are Today

While we've come a long way, I don't feel we've come nearly far enough. All of this brings me back to the topic of burnout and how it happens. Last week, I attended one of my team's retrospectives. I asked a few questions that I thought were pointed but not accusatory. I wanted to find out how I would be able to know where the team was on the path to completing certain features and functionality that had been requested and when they thought it would be done. From my perspective, it wasn't a big deal; however, it was only my perspective, and there are others to consider.

Others in the meeting thought I was being abrasive and confrontational. Being abrasive or confrontational had never been my intent. I just wanted to see that the team was striving to continue to improve and that there was ideally some way for me, as the manager, to know about what was being worked on and how long the team thought it would take to complete. But the way I was being perceived and coming across was not something the team was used to seeing. I was called out in private later, asked what was going on and why I was acting how I was. I didn't think I'd done anything wrong, but again, that was my perspective and not what everyone else was seeing. After some yelling and contemplating, I apologized to the team and continued to talk a bit with the developer who had confronted me (the same person who brought me in to take the job).

Really, this confrontation was out of concern for me. My behavior, to him, was uncharacteristic of my normal behavior. Typically, I am calm and level-headed, hard to frustrate, and not easily perturbed. He asked me a few questions about my mood, feelings, and general demeanor. My answers led him to suggest that I might have burnout because my answers apparently matched up with the symptoms on WebMD. (And yes, it also likely suggests leukemia. I'm convinced that as long as you have any symptoms at all, WebMD will provide leukemia as a potential diagnosis, so I try to avoid it.)

Burnout and YouMe

Knowing the symptoms of burnout is just a start. Wikipedia lists twelve phases of burnout and mentions that they don't necessarily happen in the order listed. Take a look and determine if you might be suffering from any of them or on a path to burnout.

1. **The compulsion to prove oneself**—This is one I definitely identify with. Between striving to be a good manager and protect the people who work with me while still attempting to show I have the coding chops to keep up with the new up-and-comers, trying to prove myself has been a constant. Taking on too much almost always follows along with this, so this one was no surprise to me.

2. **Working harder**—Again, I definitely identify with this. While I've fought very hard to make sure that no one who works for me has to work any more than 40 hours per week, I've been terrible at keeping to this for myself. I haven't done the math lately, but I'd be surprised if my *average* work week since 2006 has been much lower than 60 hours. Last

year, I worked 9-10 hours per day in the office and then went home and put in an extra ~700 hours. I've lost track of the number of times I've told employees to take their own time away from work as their own and not work on work projects while completely doing the opposite. Perhaps some of this comes from having a position where I'm essentially a full-time manager and a full-time developer. This is something I need to work on. No pun intended.

3. **Neglecting your own needs**—This one also hits close to home. I've spent uncountable evenings and weekends working when I could have been playing video games or hanging out with my wife and family. I normally don't have issues with guilt when spending time with my family, but often, playing video games or doing other activities that I enjoy has brought on a sense of guilt that I'm not spending that time being "productive" and working.

4. **Displacement of conflicts**—This is essentially being able to identify that there's a problem but not seeing the source of the problem. It may very well be where I was a week ago.

5. **Revision of values**—This is a stage where there is isolation from others and the denial of basic physical needs. Work becomes everything and all they have time for. I don't think I hit this stage, but this is likely only because my friend called me out. I can definitely see that this was where I was heading.

6. **Denial of emerging problems**—At this stage, the person suffering from burnout becomes less social and to outsiders can be seen reacting more often with sarcasm and aggression. I can see progressing quickly from one of the previous stages to this one, but I'm hoping that identifying the problem and working to correct it will prevent it from continuing into this stage.

7. **Withdrawal**—At this level, social interaction is minimized, and drugs and alcohol are often sought as coping mechanisms. Feelings of lacking hope and direction are common. Some of this does resonate.

8. **Obvious behavioral changes**—The people closest to the person suffering from burnout cannot help but notice changes in behavior. This means coworkers, family, and friends.

9. **Depersonalization**—At this level, the person starts to lose contact with him- or herself and doesn't see him- or herself or others as valuable. There is an even further lack of taking care of personal needs, and the person's actions tend to be mechanical in nature.

10. **Inner emptiness**—At this stage, there's a feeling of emptiness, and the person may try to fill this emptiness with sex, drugs, and alcohol, often to an exaggerated degree.

11. **Depression**—Often, burnout is accompanied by depression. The person is exhausted, hopeless, and indifferent and doesn't believe that there is a future for him or her. This can be extremely dangerous. Many developers tend toward some of these stages naturally with a higher-than-average number of developers falling somewhere on the Asperger's/autism spectrum, which leads to withdrawals from social interaction and often depression.

12. **Burnout syndrome**—This is an emotional and physical collapse, and the individual should seek medical attention. If depression is involved, thoughts of suicide may be involved and may be seen as the only way to escape the situation.

Clearly, burnout is a big deal. Additional side effects caused by many of these symptoms can also be a big deal. Chronic lack of sleep can lead to brain damage and the onset of Alzheimer's. Through much of my career and most of my life, I've felt that there was something big I needed to do with my life, but I've not really ever felt that I knew exactly what that is or what it looks like. I remember at twelve years old having a minor panic attack because I was already 20% of the way to being 60 and hadn't accomplished anything with my life yet.

The reality is that for almost every single one of us, nobody is going to die if our project doesn't get done this evening or this weekend. For almost all of us, nobody is going to lose his or her job. But even if that's not the case, we need to take a step back and determine if the tradeoff we are making for work is worth it. Is it worth trading away sleep now for potential brain damage or a shortened life? Is it worth giving up your life for a company or a project that is poorly managed? I don't think it is. Rushing to finish projects that were under staffed or poorly planned doesn't help anyone. It causes undue and unnecessary stress on the developers and QA testers, and it is likely to cause more bugs and errors anyway. It's amazing how many times it seems that companies don't have time to do it right in the first place, but they somehow find the time to screw it up and fix it over and over. Numerous studies have shown that working over 40 hours (and I mean just barely over, not crazy numbers) may lead to short-term gains, but continued work at that pace leads to poor software quality, more burnout, and more turnover.

So in that case, how do we burn the candle at both ends to get the understaffed and poorly planned projects done on time? I suggest that we don't. There is no safe way to burn the candle at both ends. Push for changes in the culture of your company if you're working in a situation like this. Strive for better planning and staffing a project appropriately for when they desire it to be done. It will be better for you, better for your coworkers, better for your company, and better for your project. It's not easy to bring about these changes, either, but it's worth it.

Conclusion

Many times, I see developers bragging and/or complaining about how many hours they put in during a week or how late they worked or some other extreme and dangerous behavior. Startup culture seems to be rife with these examples. Just a few days ago, I saw this quote: "I was being a bad co-founder and sleeping." Now, I don't know if this was intended facetiously or not, but I've seen messages come in from this same person at 3 or 4 in the morning, so I suspect it was serious.

We need to strive toward balance between work and the rest of our lives—myself included. If your company doesn't support sustainable practices, I encourage you to work toward change. If that's not possible, I encourage you to find a place that does support good planning and good practices. I would also like to hear your feedback and stories on this topic. Please let me know what you thought of this article and what sort of things you deal with at your job. See you next month.

Chapter

You Had One Job

David Stockton

I don't think it's much of a stretch to say that the majority of people reading this column are senior developers (or beyond) or are quickly progressing to be senior engineers. This column is primarily directed toward the senior developers or managers of senior developers. It's about how you can level up yourself, but more than that, it's about the responsibility you have in leveling up those around you. As a senior engineer, your job responsibility doesn't end at producing loads of code or being the subject matter expert on your projects.

Why This Topic?

Every month for the past 17 months or so, either I come up with a topic to write about or Oscar suggests a few and I pick from something that sounds interesting. It's not always easy to keep choosing topics and keep writing, month after month. This was one of those months until a couple of days ago, when I saw this tweet from Graham Daniels:

Graham Daniels
@greydnls

Seriously, if the mid-level and Jr developers that I work with aren't better developers after working with me then I'm not doing my job.

RETWEETS   LIKES
25   39

9:16 PM - 12 Apr 2016

4   25   39

There's so much wisdom and truth to that. If you're working as a senior developer and you're only focused on advancing yourself and your own skills, you're doing yourself, your company, and your coworkers a disservice.

What Does a Senior Developer Do?

Clearly, part of the role of a senior developer is to develop code. But that's not all. In my previous position, I worked my way up to a senior developer position. I wrote a lot of code, thought I was pretty good, and ended up as the subject matter expert on nearly every aspect of the projects I was working on. I had a few coworkers and tried to ensure that everything I was doing was clear and understood by my fellow developers.

At my current company, I came over as Director of Software Engineering, being recommended by one of the people that I had worked with previously. One of the things I'd noticed as I started interviewing candidates was the enormous range of skill level in the developers who came in to interview, even when they had the same title. Specifically, it seemed that most places promoted developers to the "Senior Developer" or "Senior Engineer" title based primarily on a certain number of years of service or experience, rather than any specific skills or responsibility they displayed. I decided early on that I wanted to establish some standards for job titles and what that meant.

My first stop was Google, trying to see if anyone else had written and shared anything regarding job titles, responsibilities, and expectations and what each level meant. I came up with nothing. Either no one had done this before, or if they did, they didn't want to share. So I decided to write my own and align my developers into the levels. By writing it all out and sharing it, the idea was that developers had a very clear indication of what it takes to move from one level to the next, of what's expected. It did mean that some people we had or that we would hire might be coming in at a "lower" job title level than they had at another company, but I wanted to ensure that at least within my company, the titles meant something.

I haven't shared this list outside of my company until now, but I feel that sharing it with you might help you out, help out your company, and help you level up. At my company, developers are expected to be performing at the level they want to be promoted to in order to be considered for promotion. We don't promote and hope that you'll eventually grow into the title; we expect you to expand your skills and responsibilities and then we upgrade your title to match what you do. The following is the list of titles and responsibilities that I came up with.

You will notice a theme among these descriptions: quality, mentoring, design, and architecture. As a developer progresses through the ranks, he or she should be producing higher quality code. Typically this translates into less code that is more flexible and has fewer bugs. This is the quality aspect. He or she should be working toward increasing the skills of their peers through teaching and helping. This is the mentoring aspect. Typically junior level developers aren't going to be asked or expected to build an application from the ground up. However, as a developer progresses, there will be a greater expectation that he or she will be able to not only understand how an application is built, but also design and architect new applications and products. Additionally, it is expected that the ability to successfully build working, maintainable software becomes more repeatable as the developer builds his or her skill set.

Software Engineering Job Levels and Responsibilities

At all levels of Software Engineering, it is expected that individuals are striving to learn and improve their craft. Suggestions for process improvements and changes that benefit the component, team, and the company are always welcome. Engineers at the lower levels are expected to learn from more senior engineers and senior engineers are expected to mentor junior engineers. Progression through the levels is not limited to certain times of year. It is expected that engineers who wish to be promoted exhibit many, if not all, of the skills and responsibilities required in the higher levels. Engineers should strive to improve themselves and their skills.

Software Development Apprentice

As a software development apprentice, you are expected to be able build simple functions, classes, and methods with supervision and heavy review. This level is reserved for developers new to development and with no real practical, real-world experience.

The developer is expected to be able to complete simple functions and methods with moderate supervision and direction. Learning about the SDLC and unit testing is also expected.

Software Developer

The Software Developer role is for those who are just starting out in the software development field. This role should be writing simple classes, methods, and functions and learning about the SDLC, including reviewing code, unit testing, documentation, and coding styles and source control. At this level, coding may be more of a "code by coincidence" than coding on purpose, but it is expected that an individual will move out of this level quickly.

The key to this level is that there is a lot of learning taking place and the individual should strive to learn as much as they can to progress to Software Engineer. Individuals at this level may have only some familiarity with a few of the components of the system they are working on.

Software Engineer

As a Software Engineer, coding is now significantly more deliberate and less "code by coincidence." The individual should be comfortable with basic unit testing concepts and be able to write simple classes, methods, and functions with some instruction but without much supervision. The individual should be paying more attention to details and beginning to emphasize development testing of their own code to eliminate all classes of obvious problems (syntax errors, invalid function calls, etc.), and should be working to increase the value their tests provide to the application. Software Engineers at this level should be quite familiar with several of the code components and possibly have advanced understanding of a few.

Senior Software Engineer

The Senior Software Engineer has an advanced knowledge of many of the components in the system and has likely written or been a key developer on several, and may be the expert in some of the components. This individual can design and develop classes, methods, and functions in a repeatable fashion and rarely writes code by coincidence. The Senior Engineer will program unit tests that are valuable in ensuring that the system is functioning properly. The Senior Engineer is developing with an emphasis on building and maintaining quality software.

The Senior Software Engineer should be able to create designs and plan for more complex interactions between classes, modules, and functions, but may still need help and supervision and review of some aspects of the design. The Senior Software Engineer will be heavily involved in reviewing other developers' code and making suggestions to ensure the quality of the final product. At this level, the engineer can take the lead role in design and development of small to medium components of the system, with the expectation that they are reviewed by peers and more senior members of the team. At this level, mentoring occurs for more junior level team members.

Staff Software Engineer

As a Staff Software Engineer, the individual will be mentoring junior developers. The focus on quality has increased beyond that of a Senior Software Engineer. Advanced unit testing, including a good understanding of mock objects and other testing concepts, is expected. The Staff Software Engineer should be able to identify and fix anti-patterns, poor development practices, and other issues that would lead to increasing technical debt.

The Staff Software Engineer is able to design and develop modules of moderate to high levels of complexity with minimal supervision. The ability to design and think through how software works is critical at this level. Staff Software Engineers are likely a lead on every project they are working on, or are involved with ensuring that Senior Software Engineers are properly leading the projects. They are responsible for ensuring quality for their team for the modules that are assigned to them.

The Staff Software Engineer has a thorough understanding of the entire system or application and is at expert level on many of the components.

Principal Software Engineer

At the Principal Software Engineer level, quality is of utmost importance. Engineers at this level are likely practicing and encouraging test-driven development with the rest of their team. They are able to plan, design, implement, and lead a team through the full Software Development Life Cycle. Unit testing is a given and identifying incorrect and useless tests by review is expected. Suggesting and implementing valuable testing procedures is required. Suggestions for problem solving and process improvement are also expected at this level. Mentoring should be continuing and Principal Software Engineers should be mentoring other mentors as well.

Researching, finding, and suggesting new software engineering practices and tools is expected. Principal Software Engineers are consistently successful in the delivery of projects and software components, as well as successfully motivating the troops. This individual is critical to the success of the projects to which they are assigned; they will also likely play an important role in design and decision making on other projects and products to which they may not be directly assigned.

Beyond Senior

As you've probably noticed, I went ahead and included two levels that go beyond the senior level, placing more emphasis on quality, mentoring, design, and architecture. I wanted to provide a path for people who are good at tech, really like doing it, and don't feel that management is the career path they want to head down. It's not uncommon at larger software companies to have an advanced tech path, and I wanted to provide it at my company as well. Too many employers see senior developers as future managers, even though they may not be good at it and may not have any interest or aptitude for management.

With Great Power...

I've outlined the responsibilities, actions, and characteristics that I would expect to see from a developer at each level. Starting out, the emphasis is on learning and improving one's own skills, and understanding how to build good software that is maintainable. Once we reach the level of Senior Software Engineer, the focus starts to shift outward, with the Senior Engineer mentoring the more junior members of the team. As I mentioned, Graham's[1] tweet was what gave me the idea for this article, but also deserving of credit was this tweet in reply from Laura Thompson:

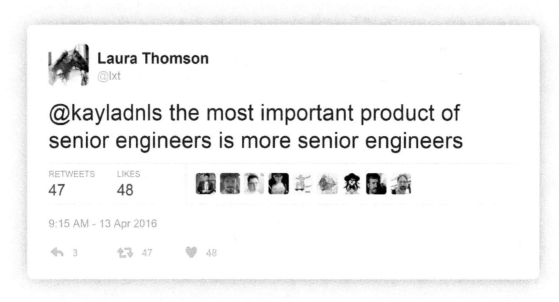

Before I continue, I want to say, if you're not following Graham (*@greydnls*) or Laura (*@lxt*), you should be.

If you're in the role of Senior Developer or Senior Engineer or something higher, your responsibility, and your challenge, is to bring up those around you. It may mean that your total output in terms of code may diminish, but that's OK. Suppose you're the Senior with eight other developers. If you produce only half the code you would have, but each of those other developers improves by 10%, it's a huge win. And the reality is that a 10% improvement of a junior developer who has a good, attentive mentor is on the low end. It's probably closer to 20–50% improvement, if not even higher. This means that mentoring is a huge win for everyone involved, from the junior mentees, the mentors, the team, and the company.

How Can You Do This?

Again, it's hard to see your code output decrease. It happens. You may be seen as your team's "rock star" developer, the go-to engineer that everyone relies on in order to get things done. It can

[1] Since publication, Grahan's twitter handle changed to @greydnls

feel good to be that lynchpin, but by holding onto knowledge, becoming that island of getting things done, you're doing yourself and others a disservice. There's a well-known term in the industry for how many (or few) people hold the critical knowledge about how the system or software works. It's called the "bus factor," and it essentially refers to how many of your developers being "hit by a bus" would bring progress to a halt.

While being a bit macabre, the "bus factor" is an important concept that needs to be understood, not just by the company, but by the developers. Being hit by a bus could just as well refer to a developer getting sick, leaving the company for another opportunity, or just taking a vacation. If you're getting a phone call when you're on the beach about how to get the message queueing system you wrote to start back up, or how to stop emails from sending because a customer messed something up, you *are* the bus factor.

Additionally, the "bus factor" can be triggered by burnout. This is typical when projects are poorly managed and result in "death marches," excessive and continued overtime, and a feeling of helplessness and despair. I wrote more about this topic in the July 2015 issue of php[architect][2], and I'd recommend you check it out if you haven't already. Burnout can become a bus factor even if the developer hasn't left the team—the quality of their code declines to the point where they are essentially making negative contributions to the project.

Some developers, sysadmins, and other IT workers like to build software in a way that's hard to understand, obfuscated, or just plain weird because they feel that if they are the only person who knows how to do something, they've got job security. The reality is that they've put themselves in the position of being the bus factor and have likely ensured they are so indispensable that they lose the chance of promotions or other career advancing opportunities, because the company cannot afford to lose them. At least for the time being. Eventually another engineer will come along and figure out what was done, why, and how to fix it, which means the original engineer will no longer be able to hold the company hostage.

Instead, I recommend working to make yourself replaceable. If you've developed new processes, code, systems, and software, and documented them well, trained up fellow developers on how everything works so that any of them can do all of it, you've opened the possibility of promotions, new projects, new opportunities, and more interesting work. And in seeing how you handle this, the developers that you're training and mentoring will see you as an example of how things ought to be done, and hopefully follow in those footsteps, training the next generation of developers to understand those systems and the new ones they create.

It's About the Mentoring

Whether you got into this industry following a degree in Computer Science or similar, or didn't go the college route and taught yourself to code, or some other path, you've got skills and ideas that others can learn and benefit from, regardless of what level of developer you are. Sharing this knowledge and teaching others is a great way to increase your own understanding

[2] *July 2015. Leveling Up: How to Burn the Candle at Both Ends:*
   https://www.phparch.com/magazine/2015-2/july/

of the topic. If you're in a senior role or above, you should be doing this already with your coworkers.

If you're not doing it already, I'd encourage instituting "lunch and learn" sessions, where a developer can teach the others about something in software, whether it's a new technique or a better explanation of the basics. If you don't have anyone who wants to present, Cal Evans offers discounts on his Nomad PHP or Day Camp 4 Developers (DC4D) video licenses for teams to help facilitate these learning sessions. Since sharing your knowledge can help others improve, you can do this even outside your company. Get involved with your local user group and give a talk. Submit a few topics you're interested in to a conference and speak about it there. You can record screen casts or Google Hangouts on Air, explaining topics and offering them for other developers to view and learn from. Blog about things you know to share your knowledge.

On freenode IRC in #phpmentoring and at *https://phpmentoring.org*, you can find a great group of people in the PHP community who have a goal of connecting mentors and mentees. Some members have these relationships in both directions, being mentored in some areas by people who are more skilled and have more knowledge in some areas, and at the same time sharing their knowledge and mentoring others in their areas of expertise.

Sometimes managers are hesitant to advocate for training for their people. I feel this is a huge mistake. Learning is vital. The following is cliché, but I feel it's completely true. The story goes that a manager is trying to justify a training budget for her developers. Her manager argues that by providing training, the developers would have better skills and be more likely to leave or be poached by recruiters. She argues back that while that is true, what happens if they never learn new things and they stay. Developers who are challenged and continuing to learn are more likely to stay in a position, all other things being equal.

Climbing By Pulling Others Up

While some individuals climb by stepping on others and pushing them down in order to gain higher ground, a much better way is to pull others up. Share your knowledge, train others, and learn new concepts with the goal of sharing that knowledge. The reason many people are senior level developers or higher is not because they've done everything right, but because they've made more mistakes and know how to recover. I'm able to help people at work sort out problems and issues quickly because chances are I've made the same mistakes in the past and can help them identify the problem and gain knowledge more quickly by avoiding those same mistakes.

Closing

Build others up, share your knowledge, present at user groups and conferences, and improve others. As a senior developer, you should be helping make others into senior developers. It will help them, it will help you, and it will improve your company, your community, and your career. See you next month.

Chapter

5

Getting the Most out of a Conference

Cal Evans

If you have never been to a PHP conference, BUY YOUR TICKET NOW! By the time this comes out the winter conference will have all opened their ticket sales and the spring conferences are right around the corner.

Last month, I wrote about how conference regulars, speakers, and organizers could make conferences friendlier to newcomers. But you don't have to wait for them to listen to me before going to your first one. The problem many first timers have is they don't know what to expect, or what to do. So, let me share with you what I've learned in ten years of being a professional conference attendee.

Know What You Want to Accomplish by Attending

OK, I hear you hollering at me "Cal, **I want to learn**!" Yes, we all do. But WHAT do you want to learn? Is there a particular problem you are trying to solve? Is there a new technique or technology you want to know more about? Even if your boss just handed you a ticket and said, go, you should put some thought into what is important to you and how you can maximize the knowledge you bring home. Look at the technologies you are using already at work, but don't limit yourself to them! If you are interested in learning about functional programming, message queues, or a new framework—that knowledge will be useful months down the road.

Review the Schedule and Select the Must See Sessions

Once you've identified what you want to learn, look at the schedule. Identify the sessions teaching what you want to learn. Identify any secondary sessions you think might be interesting. Spend a little time before you get to the conference figuring out the sessions you want to see. If the conference has an app or mobile site, check it out to see if it'll be useful. Some conferences will let you build a schedule online and send you reminders when the sessions you selected are happening.

Make a List of the People You Want to Meet

Are there speakers you want to meet or discuss a problem with? Make a list. Trust me; two days sounds like a lot of time, but it will go by fast. If you are not organized, time will slip away without you getting done what you want to get done. Speakers are usually friendly and approachable, but make sure you're not trying to meet them right before their talk. They'll appreciate a little time and space to finish preparing and getting mentally prepared to give their presentation.

Do Not Make Plans for Every Session

It is a rookie mistake to plan out every session. Keep yourself flexible. Try to leave one session each morning and every afternoon empty. If you don't fill them, you can always go to a session. However, there will be times when you get involved in a discussion with someone, you meet someone on your list and they are answering your question, or you just need to sit and digest about what you've learned so far. Leave yourself some time to think.

Don't Overdo the After Events

I get it; you paid for the ticket, and you want to squeeze every bit of goodness out of it. You want to do it all. Stop; be smart about this. There is the temptation to "go all night." Especially if you've met new people and made new friends. You want to talk, you want to share ideas, you want to keep the fun going. This feels great—until the next morning. Then, you are firing on

six out of your eight cylinders. You aren't feeling your best and you aren't performing at your peak. Be reasonable, and most importantly, if there is alcohol involved, know your limits. Know these limits going into the evening, don't try and figure them out mid-way through. Know when you want to be back in your room so you can get a reasonable amount of sleep, and if you are drinking, know how many you can have before bad decisions start to sound like good ones.

Take and Share Notes

Find a way to take notes that will be useful for you later. You should share these via a blog post, ideally. Your team back home might learn a thing or two from your notes, and just the act of explaining and teaching them what you learn will solidify your understanding. Finally, when it comes time to rate the talks (and speaker's really appreciate honest, constructive feedback) your notes can help you remember the talk and explain how it could be improved.

Make Time for Yourself

Finally, make sure you are having a good time. Don't let the pressure of having to fill every minute, having to meet everyone on your list, or having to attend every after-hours event suck all the life out of the event for you. Part of what I get out of conferences is a chance to get away from it all while still being immersed in tech. I can focus on tech but still take the time to reflect on where I am, where my career is, and where things are going. Make time for self-inspection and reflection. To get the most out of the conference, you should come back informed and energized. It should be a time to recharge your batteries, as much as it is a time to get inspired by new technologies and now tools. And, depending on expectations back at work, you may need some time to answer emails from your boss and colleagues who are covering for you while you learn.

Conferences are great! If you have never been to one, make an effort to get to one next year. Your career will thank you.

Chapter 6

PHP Conference Newbies 101

Trip Witt

10 Ways to Maximize Your First Experience

> *"You take the blue pill—the story ends, you wake up in your bed and believe whatever you want to believe. You take the red pill—you stay in Wonderland, and I show you how deep the rabbit hole goes. Remember: all I'm offering is the truth. Nothing more."*
>
> – *The Matrix*

So, you decided to take the red pill. You are planning to attend your first PHP conference, or perhaps you are trying to convince your company to send you. Maybe your company is unsure of what you will get out of it. Or maybe you're still unsure of how any of the experiences as an attendee will affect your day-to-day programming.

In May 2014, without knowing what Laravel or Magento even were, I took the "red pill." I stepped out of my comfortable cave and opened my eyes to the bright new world of a PHP developer-driven event by attending php[tek]. Attending a PHP conference is something I had envisioned doing for a long time. Here are 10 lessons I think first-time attendees should know, to maximize the experience as they attend their first PHP conference.

Lesson 1: You Are Neither the Dumbest nor the Smartest Person in the Room

I don't mean to sound politically incorrect; however, this first lesson kept me from attending a conference or speaking up at local PHP groups in the first place. I didn't want to be that person with the least amount of experience in a conference room full of PHP developers. Neither did I want to sit next to someone who was smug about anything and everything.

I learned immediately that a PHP conference is for everyone. Not a single brilliant mind diminished my programming skill set. Instead, other developers led me to learn new techniques and coding practices. I was able to add value by doing the same with others in turn. Whether it was helping debug another's application or reiterating a concept I had learned myself, I was still able to contribute.

There is a certain mindset at PHP conferences. PHP conferences are a community of fellow developers. We all struggle. We contribute to each other's successes by listening and sharing our own experiences. By being together, we can all create truly better applications and indulge in better discussions to benefit our programming future.

Lesson 2: Speak Up

Just because the speaker said something one way and Chuck gets it, doesn't mean that everyone will understand it the same way. If you don't understand something, raise your hand and ask. If you still struggle, ask someone else. More often than not, someone in attendance is willing to come up to you and help. Making yourself heard at a PHP conference is also your opportunity to receive unbiased help. Lastly, speaking up can lead to new friendships, localized PHP communities, or a new RFC in the PHP core itself.

Lesson 3: How to Get a Free Pound of Bacon—Meeting the Conference Organizers and Speakers

The conference organizers put a lot of time, talent, and energy into pulling off the great event. You can usually recognize them by their conference T-shirts. Speak with them, know their story, and thank all of them for their efforts. These organizers believe so wholeheartedly in the PHP community that they are willing to commit a large part of their lives to organizing developers from all backgrounds as a way to contribute to the greater good of the developer community and give you an experience where you can get involved and immerse yourself in the programming world you love.

But let's say you don't see something you like. If you think something should be added to the program, say so. If you would like to see a tutorial in a future event, ask! Even if it's as small as the menu lacking the food you love, whine!

For example: I'm a big fan of bacon. And nowhere on the breakfast spread could I find bacon! So, I took Lesson 2 to heart and spoke up about my concern over the lack of sliced bovine to one of the conference organizers. Believe it or not… the next day I had a hotel voucher for a free pound of bacon.

That exchange became an ice breaker for me and an excellent way to make new friends and feel more comfortable at the event. This one little thing made such a difference to me and inevitably became my favorite story to share with other attendees.

As a side note, don't forget to have a discussion with the speakers themselves. Discover new trends and techniques and then take it to the next level by conversing with the speaker. You may be surprised by what you find out or what you have been missing out on. Having a discussion with a Magento evangelist was invaluable to me, even though the framework didn't apply to me or my company.

Lesson 4: Here, There, and Everywhere—Attending Events and Making the Most of the Schedule

The number of speakers and interests the organizers gather together in one conference is unbelievable. The organizers put out a call for papers and pore over all of the submissions to give the attendees the best experience possible. With that being said, it is impossible to get to everything the event has to offer.

A few pieces of time management advice. If you have a timing conflict with one speaker over another, attend the speaker you know less about first and the speaker you know more about last. Here's why. In my experience, midway through the speech of the subject you know least about, the material becomes overwhelming. The speech with the subject you thought you knew more about suddenly starts giving you tidbits of information you didn't know. This method gives the best of both worlds. And, sometimes it's worth skipping both sessions to have a discussion with a previous speaker or a group of other attendees about something that pertains to you more than what is currently scheduled.

Lesson 5: Be Prepared

I was nervous at my first PHP conference. I let anxiety get the best of me and put off reading up on the topics that would be discussed. I was familiar with PHP 5.3 but had not yet incorporated 5.4 or above. I hadn't explored namespaces, frameworks (except my own), or even Composer, for that matter. Do yourself a favor and create virtual environments on your host machine to suit each and every one one of these topics. Spend some time covering the basics of them. Set up a 'hello world' application. Most of the speakers will always refer to the markup, and it will help to know what they all do and how to use them. Don't let the easy stuff weigh you down. A rudimentary understanding of these programming interfaces will go a long way in speaker presentations and accompany discussions with new friends.

Lesson 6: Know Your Frameworks...

At the introduction of this article, I mentioned stepping out of a cave. This is where that analogy comes into play. There are so many frameworks, each tailored to eradicate duplicity and ease the coding process for PHP developers. The frameworks alone could justify a whole convention by themselves. Because there are so many frameworks and programming-specific markups, it can be very tricky to understand the role each framework plays. Refer to Lesson 5, and go through the basics of just being prepared to be "in the know." If one of them is of interest, you and your company can benefit from their utilities, and the conference will pay for itself through the knowledge you will learn from framework evangelists.

Lesson 7: Know Your Bartender—How to Get Around in the City

This may not seem like a real lesson, but it is. Going to a PHP conference isn't all about education and learning. It's about having fun, too. When you travel to a big city and you are in a conference hotel, it's easy to become isolated from the world. Go out and explore the big city you are visiting. This area of discussion leads me to a critical component of attending a conference. There is no one with more knowledge than the bartender at a hotel lounge. Besides knowing the city in his or her own right, the bartender has heard the stories of all the hotel patrons who have visited the area.

Bartenders can help you get from the conference to the sights and attractions and back in time so you'll never miss a beat. And it's OK if you miss a speaker session to see the big city. This is what developing yourself all is about, too. The bartender in my situation helped me get from the second- to-last session at the hotel to Millennium Park in Chicago and back, all in less than three hours. He arranged the hotel shuttle to coincide with the train and told me when I needed to be back on the train to make it to the evening events. I could not thank him enough. If you want to spend more time, it's up to you.

I'm not saying this method is for everyone. I was on a self-imposed tight schedule. A better way of going about visiting the city would be to announce your intentions and gather more attendees who are interested by using Twitter or Facebook. Round up as many as you can and head out into the city together. The more the merrier, and the more likely you are to have an even greater experience.

Lesson 8: Sponsors

I come from a PHP developer world where "the cloud" cannot exist. With that being said, the sponsors that you meet will become your best friends for various individual and corporate reasons. They all have something to offer each of the attendees and their marketing material is aimed right at us. Whether we want to score our code, develop inside of a profound framework, or support and mentor women worldwide through PHP Women, they all have something unique to offer that can be applied to your aptitude and daily development artillery. Not to mention the free T-shirts.

Lesson 9: Leave Work at Work

From my limited prior experience and co-attendees' points of view, the further away you are from work, the better. It seems the closer you are to work, the more available you are to facilitate their needs. My company is very understanding, the backbone of my attendance and the financer of my first PHP conference. Remember, you are there to gain insight into the company's needs and supplement your education for them. Getting away from work clears your mind and can create a sharper focus for tomorrow's efforts.

Lesson 10: Come Back—the Return of the Attendee

I hope you'll take the red pill and enjoy your first PHP conference. You can create your own PHP help desk of new friends, participate in discussions that interest you, and learn new tricks to add to your arsenal. Returning to a future conference is just as important as attending the very first one, too. You will probably see some familiar faces, and you will also remain current in the development community.

Going to conferences can also spur your interest in taking part in the event itself. Perhaps you want to take your attendance one step further and submit a paper so you can speak at a future conference. Maybe you'll even start your own user group in your community. Or just come back and participate more as an attendee. The whole idea is just to come back, whether you re-attend a conference or visit a difference conference. Never stop networking and never stop making friends in the PHP community.

Web technology is changing and never stands still. New timesaving features, enhancements in server hardware, and the never-ending RFCs to the core of PHP are just a few pieces of the larger puzzle that PHP developers are working towards solving. It's up to you to stay current with the new trends. Regularly attending conferences is a way of "sharpening the saw" to remain cutting edge yourself.

Whatever path you choose, I encourage all of you to take your skill set to the next level. Join a local PHP community or create your own. You can do this all by yourself in your own comfortable cave, but it is a lot more fun and engaging to go to your first conference and participate in a greater experience amongst fellow developers.

Side Bar—from the Boss

We asked the author to include his boss' perspective.

As a manager you should ask yourself, "Why is this employee valuable, and how did they become valuable?" The answer in most technical employees can be summed up in two words: knowledge and application. So the next question naturally becomes, "How do we get more of 'that stuff' to increase productivity/value?" The point I am driving at is simple: if you invest in developing your IT staff you will make more money/meaning through them.

Knowledge and application of that knowledge is really only gained from experience. As humans we can learn from other people's experiences, so it just naturally makes sense to connect your team into a network of professionals to learn what works, what doesn't, and what could be done differently. It's also an opportunity for your team to share experiences and get true peer reviews of their solutions in a non-threatening setting. Frankly, there is so much "win" here, it's hard to put any other value on it than "priceless." While what others have done can teach your team a lot, it's what people WILL do in the future that can give you the greatest edge.

The I.T. landscape changes quickly. To remain relevant and competitive, a company must keep up. To be a world leader, a company must not only keep up, but apply the changes internally. In all cases, you need to keep your team briefed on changes in technology at the earliest possible opportunity. Conferences like this are a great venue for innovators to introduce their technology—so by having your team in attendance you can effectively get the "inside scoop" on what's to come. Because ideas also flow effortlessly between people, your team at the same time can brainstorm with other professionals, jump starting your own development process. The multiples created by these synergies are insane.

So why do I send my team to quality events? Because I selfishly want to be able to rely on the biggest, most powerful arsenal of people to help me attain my goals for the company and make meaning in the world. I truly believe that everyone has "super powers"—but those powers have to be encouraged to grow and be refined. Conferences are simply one of the best ways to do this for open source web application developers. Superheroes make my world a better place.

Chapter

7

Fear of Public Speaking

Joe Devon

I don't feel comfortable writing about this, so I'll take it as a sign that I should go out of my comfort zone and share it.

Some people are shocked when I say I have a fear of public speaking. That's because I've been running tech events for about seven years. I'm on lots of panels, in front of hundreds of people sometimes. So I'll explain in the hope of inspiring others.

My fear came about when I did a college debate, screwed up a joke that didn't get laughs, and just basically bombed. I don't know why, but it put a bug in my head and made me shy about public speaking from then on.

That wasn't my only fear: I grew up with others, and they probably all mix together to create anxiety. My father always had ice water in his veins—which is understandable, as he survived Auschwitz and Dachau. If you can face the SS and survive, what else could scare you?

My mom, on the other hand, was a big ball of fear. In my opinion, this came about because she was hidden in the free part of France during World War II. She used to go up and down the mountain collecting fruit to feed the family, who were hiding in the cellar of a blessed French Christian family for the duration of the war.

There were many occasions when people in the surrounding area would threaten to tell the Nazis that my mom's family was hiding. It was terrifying, because even the free part of France hadn't escaped anti-Jewish sentiment. There's a lot more to tell, but that's another story for another day.

I mention this because as a child, things like dealing with authority figures provided a fascinating view into contrasts. My mom would freak out in all of these situations—approaching a border, when police were around, being stopped for a ticket—and that fear was passed along to me. It took me years to be able to handle the anxiety of crossing a border, and I still feel it sometimes.

On the other hand, my dad was always as cool as a cucumber. Even when he once came home from getting mugged at gunpoint, he handled it with cool. When a doctor faced my dad and told him that he wasn't going to survive his cancer, my dad took it well, causing the heretofore emotionless doctor to break down in tears. He couldn't believe how well my dad took it. Dad just said, "This isn't the first time I've faced death or been told I wouldn't live long."

Face the Fear

In spite of nameless, faceless fear, I always secretly dreamed of being able to do a speech in public, with the ultimate being a keynote talk. Less than a decade ago, this seemed like a fantasy, but I took baby steps.

The first step was to start organizing meetups. I did that, but—and this is hard to admit—I was terrified of introducing speakers at first. I remember having a Facebook DBA speak via Skype and happily passing along the task of the introduction to someone else.

But I kept at it, kept doing events, and started introducing people. I got more comfortable with it. Once in a while I had a little shortness of breath, but if anyone noticed, they didn't say a word. And frankly, who cares?

Invitation to Speak on a Panel

Then the moment of truth came. I was invited to speak on a panel at the Semtech conference in front of 150-250 people. Oh my God—that was truly scary! Five minutes before the talk, I went to the bathroom and almost threw up. Then I went to the podium and cursed myself for accepting the offer: what an idiot I was! But I pushed through and took the advice of a friend who had done a fair bit of theater. He said: "Keep your feet flat on the ground the whole time, it makes you feel grounded." Amazingly, that helped, and once I got through the first few seconds, I felt great. I just loved that panel!

Impostor Syndrome

I guess I did well enough, as the conference owner started inviting me to more panels, to close out his NoSQL conference several years running. Each year it got easier. But still, it feels quite funny to sit next to world-class experts and to have folks in the audience who invented the protocols being discussed asking my opinion on things. But I was determined not to say no and to face my fear.

Are These Just Words?

I'm positive that these fears are common in our industry. I see anxiety in the eyes of seasoned, well-respected speakers sometimes. It's all about getting past the first few seconds or moments with shortness of breath, so those who haven't made the jump are sure to feel the same way. I'm sure many readers might look at this and think: "Yeah, those are just words, but he doesn't feel overwhelming anxiety as strongly as I do." Trust me, I do.

Chewing Gum and Other Tricks

So, having shared this, let me also tell you a couple of tricks of the trade. Chew gum. Really. Your body will not go into the fight-or-flight response if you're chewing gum and your body is working on digestive juices. Your body knows that if you're eating, you aren't worried about a predator hunting you down for an easy meal. And as mentioned earlier, plant your feet firmly on the ground. It works! Another one is to postpone the anxiety. Don't freak out a week before the event. Tell yourself you're "allowed" to feel the fear only 10 minutes before you speak. This minimizes the impact.

A whole organization sprouted up to help speakers face their fear: Toastmasters. There are tons of them! Join one and try it out—I did.

Is Everyone Looking at Me?

One of the reasons people get stage fright is a biological response. If you're standing out on the plains and every creature's face is eyeing you, you might just be food. Time to run!!!

Culmination of a Dream

I'm happy to report that I survived and achieved my dream. I was invited to keynote MidwestPHP (*http://2015.midwestphp.org*) and managed to overcome my nerves and deliver the talk.

It was nerve-wracking, and I was concerned my talk wasn't good enough. At the speakers' dinner the night before, I heard from an established speaker about her first keynote and how rough it was, which just served to freak me out some more. I did a dry run in my room, and it didn't go well. I didn't like the talk and even reworked it that night.

Next day, when finding out where the talk would take place, it turned out it was a room where every single seat was built to point to the podium, similar to what you see in the movie The Paper Chase. Oy vey!

In fact, at one point I froze and couldn't think. So I simply shared that I was a little nervous as it was my first keynote, and that calmed me down and I could move along. Despite all the anxiety, I averaged 5 stars on JoindIn (*http://j.mp/midkeynt*), and many people came up to tell me how much they enjoyed the talk and learned. So the anxiety was unwarranted.

I hope sharing the process of facing my fears inspires those of you in the same boat to take the same path. Please drop me a note if this helps. It will make me feel very good :)

What Was the Talk About?

OK, we're done talking about anxiety, so let's share the topic of the talk. It was accessibility.

As regular php[architect] readers know, I co-founded an event called GAAD (Global Accessibility Awareness Day—*http://GlobalAccessibilityAwarenessDay.org*). It's a day meant to build awareness about accessibility for developers, designers, and everyone dealing with digital technology. We need to build things so that they are available to folks with disabilities.

My talk was a brief history of the founding of GAAD, followed by some videos and examples of how the way we code can harm the ability of assistive devices such as screen readers to access websites.

If you're not aware of accessibility, please do some research and participate in GAAD on May 21 this year. There's more to come in next month's php[architect].

Spreading Awareness of Accessibility

Considering the topic, I was happy and quite surprised at how well my keynote talk was received. Four of the five blog posts recapping the event mentioned that they were surprised to see the videos of assistive technology in action, and that they would put more effort into doing a better job in the future. Many folks reached out to me about improving their internal processes, and some reached out to the core developers working on their favorite open source framework or project.

It was a great wake-up call. It made me aware that much more work needs to be done—but also that I was right that if people just knew the harm their code was causing, they would put in more effort.

I plan to redouble my efforts, and you'll see more about that soon.

What Else Happened at Midwest PHP?

Beth Tucker Long, a former php[architect] editor-in-chief, made a great presentation about diversity and women in tech. Empathy begins when you put yourself in someone else's shoes, and Beth provided several examples of insensitive comments, to say the least, that she's had to face when speaking at a conference. For example, if she came with her husband, people assumed she was tagging along for his conference. That's quite disrespectful for someone of Beth's chops and accomplishments.

There were harsher examples, but considering how stressful it can be to speak, can you imagine how undermining subtle digs like that can be? And when it's from well-meaning people, sometimes that's even worse. I've learned a lot by asking women in tech about their experiences. After her presentation, Beth was joined by Eryn O'Neil and Gary Hokin for a great panel about the topic.

We also had a spirited developer panel led by Nate Abele. Topics ranged from licenses to finding Cobol coders to tech lobbies and the EFF. It was wonderful to see a room full of so many super-smart people.

Elizabeth Marie Smith closed the conference with an amazing and provocative keynote. She urged people to contribute back to open source projects—or else you're a thief. I posted that comment to Facebook and got quite a backlash :) But her point was that if you use open source, it's only fair to help out. You don't have to write C code to give back. You can help core developers by simply engaging the community: volunteer at or run a meetup, answer questions in the project's IRC, help with the documentation. There are lots of ways to contribute!

My favorite part of the conference was hanging out with such a great group of people. I've seen Dave Stokes at many conferences, but this time he shared some fascinating stories. I hope that one day he'll turn that into a talk, even if it isn't all directly related to code. And kudos to Jonathan Sundquist for running such a great conference and also for working on doing a GAAD event this year in Minnesota.

Chapter 8

Two Years of PHPAmersfoort: Running a Local Usergroup

Stefan Koopmanschap

Two years ago as of this writing, we organized the first meeting of PHPAmersfoort[1], the local PHP usergroup for the city of Amersfoort in The Netherlands. It has been a very interesting time filled with lessons on how to run a local usergroup and discovering what works and what doesn't, with a great number of speakers presenting and many intriguing discussions. In this article, I want to share with you some of the things we've learned along the way and give you some tips and tricks for running your own local usergroup.

[1] PHPAmersfoort—http://phpamersfoort.nl

Our Start

The Dutch are lazy—hold on, I'll explain. I was talking to Michelangelo van Dam of PHPBenelux while at the php[tek] conference, and he told us the difference that PHPBenelux sees between its meetings in Belgium and its meetings in The Netherlands in terms of attendance is huge. The Belgian meetings regularly have 50+ people attending, while only about 20 people attend the Dutch meetings. One of the reasons for this is that the Dutch are not willing to travel: If they need to travel for more than 20-30 minutes to a usergroup meeting, they'd rather stay home.

It wasn't a huge surprise that when Rafael Dohms started the first local usergroup in Amsterdam, it became an instant success. After AmsterdamPHP took off, slowly more and more local usergroups began popping up. Rotterdam, Zoetermeer, Groningen, Twente, an ever-increasing number arose.

While this was happening, Jelrik van Hal, Richard Tuin, and I worked together on a project at Enrise. At some point, the three of us started saying (in jest) that it would be nice if Amersfoort also had a usergroup. I'd love to say we started working on it and that the next month there was a

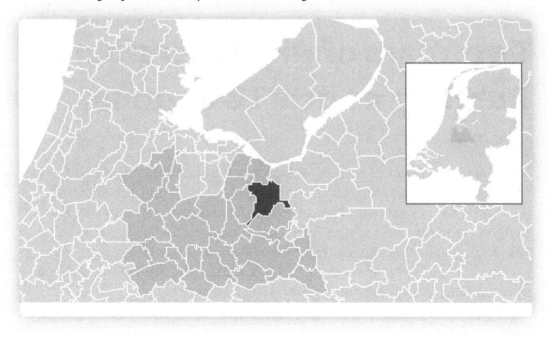

meeting, but I'd be lying. It took a couple of similar lunch meetings before we decided to publish our plans. We called for people from Amersfoort to come together to brainstorm, and we set our goals, picked a specific day of the month (the second Tuesday of the month) for our meet ups, and off we went: August 13, 2013, saw the inaugural meet up at Seats2Meet in Amersfoort, with Harrie Verveer speaking about PHPUnit.

Preparing a Plan

We created a plan on what we wanted to do and achieve with PHPAmersfoort. In an informal group like this, that was a great idea. Every idea we have and every speaker we might be able to get—we can easily test whether this is according to plan. Such a plan ensures we can stay focused on what we need to do: organize meet ups. It ensures things don't immediately become chaotic.

First of all, we had two goals:

- Be a meeting place outside the workplace for PHP developers and people interested in PHP in the Amersfoort area
- Facilitate the sharing of knowledge by providing a technical talk with attendees

Not every meet up needed to adhere to both of the above goals. For instance, we've organized meet ups without a speaker, where we'd go and play lasertag. And last year, as our birthday celebration, we organized a bowling night as part of our regular meet up. However, everything we organize should meet at least one of our goals.

Stick to the Plan?

A plan is nice but, obviously, you need to be flexible and realistic. We found out quickly that not many people liked the lasertag meet ups. Therefore, we stopped planning those. Organizing a meet up, even if it's just to play lasertag, takes effort. If the meet up ends up bringing together the same small group of five or six people, it's a bit useless to keep doing what you're doing. We still play lasertag every once in a while, but it's no longer part of PHPAmersfoort.

Tools We Use

Once you've got a plan, you need to actually start doing work. We've found a set of tools with PHPAmersfoort that really work for us.

Meetup.com

Meetup.com[2] is a great tool for organizing meetings. It offers an event management and registration system, but it also offers a huge userbase. When you start your Meetup group, Meetup.com automatically e-mails people in your area who are interested in your group's topic. This is great help for finding an initial group of people.

Meetup.com has a monthly fee to use its service, but it's not a lot of money. This fee can either be paid by the organizers or be covered by a sponsor. In our case, we found a sponsor willing to pay.

I must be honest though: Lately meetup.com has been removing some really useful features. First it removed the check-in option in which attendees could "check in" to a meetup when they were there. More recently, it removed the "sponsor perks" feature, which was a great way for sponsors to promote themselves in the Meetup group: they could give a discount code to members for instance. While we never really used the check-in feature (I know AmsterdamPHP

[2] Meetup.com—*http://meetup.com*

did though for its raffler software), the sponsor perks are our way of communicating some cool discounts to our members. We need to find a new to do this. It is important to keep looking at the tools you use to see whether they're still effective for what you use them for. If a better alternative to Meetup.com becomes available, we'll likely switch.

Google Drive

We have quite a few documents that we might need to work on together. We've got documents listing potential speakers and potential venues and, of course, we have our schedule for the upcoming meet ups. To easily share these documents and also work on them collaboratively, we've found Google Drive/Google Docs to be a great tool. That way, we'll never lose data when someone saves a document should someone else also be working on it.

Joind.in

In the PHP community, this is an obvious tool used to gather feedback on the speaker and meet up. Every meet up gets created on joind.in, and attendees are asked to leave feedback on the speaker and the event on the joind.in[3] site. This is also good for (starting) speakers, because many conference organizers check feedback on joind.in when selecting talks for their conference.

Slack

We have our own private Slack[4]-network where we talk to each other, discuss potential

[3] Joind.in—http://joind.in
[4] Slack—http://slack.com

speakers and locations, and generally get things sorted. When we started, we were all in the same office, but this is not always the case now depending on the projects we work on and the clients we work for.

We used to use Skype for this, with a dedicated PHPAmersfoort chat, but we've migrated to Slack. The option of having different channels is useful, and because we all use Slack for some other projects and communities as well, it seemed like a good replacement for Skype.

Trello

Because discussing and assigning tasks in a chat sometimes resulted in those tasks not getting done, we needed a simple tool to keep track of tasks, who is working on a task, and what the task's status is. For this, Trello[5] got introduced. Trello is a very easy-to-use tool that serves as something of a Kanban-board to keep track of tasks.

WhatsApp

We don't use WhatsApp a great deal, but we do have a group chat for the occasional item that arises when we're not at a computer.

---

[5] Trello—http://trello.com

Funding the Group

In an informal group like this, money is an obvious problem. While all founding members were very happy to invest in the starting of the group, consistently paying for venues, coffee and tea, snacks, soda, and beer is a bit much. There are a lot of ways to avoid the need to spend money on organizing a usergroup (I'll get back to that later), but there are some things that cost money regardless. It's good to have some sponsors who can help you out. For PHPAmersfoort, we've got ServerGrove sponsoring our website, but there are several hosting websites out there willing to donate hosting for usergroups. Ingewikkeld, my company, is paying for the Meetup. com account and pays for some things that pop up every now and then. We even had a member who stepped up to pay for the cost of one of the meet ups at some point, which is really incredible.

One thing we wanted to prevent was needing to ask our members to pay for attending the meet up. One of the charms of local usergroups is that people are free to come by whenever they want to, regardless of their financial position or whether a boss wanted to pay for them to attend. So far, in our two years of running the usergroup, we have never had to charge for the meet up.

How do you run a usergroup without spending money? By getting yourself sponsors.

What are the Costs of a Usergroup

The list of things that cost money for a usergroup is not that long. Our list of costs is as follows:

- Website hosting
- Meetup.com
- Venues
- Coffee and tea
- Drinks and snacks

As mentioned before, ServerGrove graciously offered to host our website (as it does with many usergroups), and we have a sponsor for the Meetup.com fees, so the only costs we need to cover are related to the meet ups we organize.

Our Sponsor Proposition

We try to have all the costs related to a meet up be covered by the same sponsor. This is for a very simple reason: it saves us work. We prefer to have a meet up hosted by our sponsor. This basically means that the sponsor provides us with a room where the meet up can take place in addition to coffee/tea before the speaker presents and drinks and snacks afterward. Usually, this means that our meet ups occur in the sponsor's office. This is an excellent situation for both parties: We get to have a good venue, usually with wifi as well, where we can meet, and the sponsor is able to show attendees his or her company.

The main reason for companies to sponsor a meet up is recruiting. I know very few companies doing PHP right now that are not looking for more developers. This is great because that means there are enough companies willing to sponsor meet ups, but we do have some rules. Sponsors can, if they want, introduce themselves quickly at the start of the meet up. We give them 5–10 minutes to do so if they want. We will also put their logo on our opening and closing slides. And of course, they can put flyers or other promotional materials in their office. We discourage actively recruiting attendees however. This is both to prevent our attendees from annoying recruitment attempts but also to protect our sponsor from getting a bad reputation. If someone is looking for a job, he or she will approach the sponsor if interested in a position. In a world where most developers get approached by recruiters nearly daily, having that happen at a meet up is a pretty quick way to never see that attendee at a meet up ever again.

Sometimes we get sponsors who have no office in the Amersfoort region. They usually just pay for us to rent a room and get some drinks. If possible, we ask them to arrange the room for us or at least give an OK on being invoiced directly by the venue where we rent the room so that we don't have to pay for it and then try to get our money reimbursed by the sponsor. We want to minimize our financial risk and our involvement. It takes enough time to organize everything already.

Finding Venues

As mentioned before, the venues are usually simply the sponsor's office building. There are not many requirements for the venue. The most important item we need is a projector and of course enough room to accommodate the attendees. We average about 20-25 people, so we usually aim for a venue that has room for 25-30. We always do ask for the capacity upfront so we can put a maximum capacity on Meetup.com. This prevents a greater number of people coming to the event than the venue can hold.

Aside from needing the projector and enough chairs for attendees, we prefer our venue to be easily accessible by both car and public transportation. This doesn't always work out well, but most of the venues we use these days are pretty easy to reach. Of course because we're a local usergroup, attendees are mostly local anyway, so a simple bikeride is not a big problem for most.

Getting Speakers

Getting speakers for a usergroup can be a challenge, especially when you're not in an area where many regular speakers reside. As such, when we first began the usergroup, we decided to host some speakers from other parts of the country. Thanks to the fact that all of the crew are active in the Dutch and international PHP community, we have many speakers we can e-mail.

From the start, however, we have been promoting the usergroup as a place for new speakers to get some experience. Over the past two years, we've had several new or relatively new speakers giving their talks at PHPAmersfoort to get some more experience. All of these talks have been terrific, and the feedback the speakers received on joind.in was also very positive. The speakers have also received some constructive comments on how to improve their talks. This is exactly why usergroups are a good place for beginning speakers.

As a usergroup organizer, you should also be aware of bigger events going on in your country or region. If there are conferences in your own region or in your country, chances are you could get a speaker to come over to your usergroup to deliver a talk. We have not really been able to get international speakers to PHPAmersfoort because the timing has not worked, but several other Dutch usergroups have had international speakers present at their meet ups. These were usually much better attended than regular meet ups are, and they are excellent advertisements for your usergroup!

Another reason to keep an eye on conferences is that you can spot local, regional, or national speaking talent. PHPAmersfoort recently had Jakub Gadkowski, who did a talk at the Dutch PHP Conference Uncon, and was so good that he immediately was invited to PHPAmersfoort, where he repeated his talk and received fantastic feedback.

One thing to make very clear is that we do not offer speakers any compensation for their presenting at our usergroup. Because we don't have any income, we can't really give anything in return for a presentation. So far though, we haven't had any speakers expecting any compensation; it is part of the usergroup ecosystem that people don't get (or even expect) compensation for speaking. If you're starting a local usergroup, don't worry about compensation; it really isn't necessary.

Meet-up Logistics

All the previous is mostly about preparations and organization, but how does an actual meet up work? We always publish the schedule upfront so people know what to expect, and the schedule is much the same every month:

      7:00 p.m. - Welcome with coffee/tea
      7:30 p.m. - Opening by PHPAmersfoort crew
      7:35 p.m. - Speaker
      8:30 p.m. - Closing by PHPAmersfoort, possible raffle
      8:40 p.m. - Drinks and snacks

After experiencing different schedules at different usergroups, we decided with PHPAmersfoort to only have one speaker per meet up. This gives attendees a good reason to come to the meet up to learn something, but also gives enough time for socializing and getting to know each other. An important part of the meet up is not just the learning but also the social interaction among attendees. Whether it is for business purposes (developers might just find their next job at the meet up) or simply for pleasure (chances are, there are people with similar hobbies or interests at the meet up), this interaction is valuable. Some usergroups choose to host two speakers and have mingling time afterward, but we've found that most people also want to try to be home relatively early. Most meet ups end around 10 p.m., although we've had nights when people had such a good time that it was quite late before the last people said their good-byes.

We usually try to be at the venue 15–30 minutes in advance. The first attendees generally arrive 5-10 minutes before the meet up officially starts, and you want to have some time to set everything up (or help the sponsor set everything up). We also stay a bit after the last person leaves to help clean things up a bit. This is a courtesy for your sponsors, and we hope this ensures they will want to invite you back for another meet up at their offices.

Special Activities

As mentioned before, we've had some special activities. These were either combined with a normal meet up or just organized as a seperate event. The venue that we usually rent when the sponsor doesn't have an office in Amersfoort has several options for this. As such, we've rented some bowling alleys a couple of times and we've gone to play laser tag.

Early in the usergroup's history, we combined these activities with a regular meet up, but we found that if we'd go bowling or play lasertag after the speaker was done, we'd lose several of our regular visitors. They'd just go home because they weren't interested in participating.

An exception to that rule was our first anniversary, when we announced upfront that there would be bowling after the regular meet up was done. We had found a sponsor for this activity so that people wouldn't have to spend their own hard-earned money on it. The number of people staying after the regular meet up was much higher, and we celebrated our first anniversary with an excited group of developers playing bowling. Much fun was had.

The Crew

As the crew members, you're the steady part of the group. Every meet up, there's (usually) a different group of people (with a bunch of regulars coming to most meet ups). But even changes can happen within the crew. We expanded the crew with Rick Kuipers after a while. Rick was one of our hardcore regulars and was very willing to help, so we invited him to join the team. This worked out really well.

People sometimes also change. Life changes, and situations change. A couple of months ago, I stepped back from the PHPAmersfoort crew. I just had too much going on, both personally and with business, so I couldn't commit to the work needed for PHPAmersfoort. I still visit most of the meet ups though.

Your organizing crew will change over time. You should be proactive in managing it. Keep an eye on regulars who could be encouraged to step up and help when others decide they no longer can.

Starting Your Own Usergroup

All of what is mentioned above is the story of PHPAmersfoort, the first local usergroup I've been involved with. But how do you go about beginning your own story? As the great Cal Evans always says:

"If you have no local usergroup, you ARE the local usergroup."

Let's get started! Because organizing everything by yourself is a great deal of work, finding one or two like-minded people to help you out is a great idea. Get yourself the right set of tools needed to organize meet ups, set a date, and get a speaker, and you'll be on your way to your first birthday as a usergroup. Don't forget to register yourself as *http://php.ug*! And remember: Find your own way. What worked for us in Amersfoort may not work for your situation. As such, get moving and start your own story!

Chapter 9

Finding the Solution to the Problem

David Stockton

As software developers or engineers, our job is not to write code. In fact, we should be writing as little code as we can. Every line of code we write is a liability: a potential security hole, a new bug, a tight coupling that makes future modifications difficult or impossible. It may surprise you to realize that writing code isn't even what your job is about.

As a software engineer (I'm not getting into the debate about whether anything we do with software can truly be considered "engineering," but bear with me), with very few exceptions, we are problem-solvers. We need to hear or read a description of what is needed and figure out how to make it happen in code. Except instead of jumping straight into our editor and banging out code that we think does what is asked for, we often should take it further and ask questions. Many times, we are given a task and expected to blindly follow and do what it says—the proverbial and (now) somewhat derogatory "code monkey" tasks. "Move the button down 4 pixels, change the asterisk to a different shade of green, make these 100 PDF reports output as a single report with 100 pages." Each of these requests has a different motivation, and the people requesting them may well have good intentions. But let's take a further look.

Request for Changes

A request to move a button around on the page is simple, right? Just* change the top CSS property or use any of numerous possible ways to move things around. But why? Perhaps where it is doesn't align with other buttons on the same line and makes things look unprofessional. So how about changing the framework to make it easier to ensure everything is aligned properly? Suddenly the solution may not be as simple, but it could be more robust and actually save time in the long run. Or it could be that the button just needs to move down 4 pixels because it is afraid of heights.

> * *"Just" is a very dangerous word. It implies simplicity and a completely thorough understanding of the problem. I recommend calling out usages of "just" whenever you hear them. "Oh, it's 'just' a simple change," "It's 'just' some CSS," "It's 'just' a drawn reciprocating dingle arm to reduce sinusoidal depleneration," etc. Until the change has been completed and tested and marked as done, we really don't know what it "just" was. Is it possible that it's simple? Sure, absolutely. But the people making the change are nearly always in a better position to make the call about what it "just" is, and even then, it may not be that great a position. Avoid using the word "just" in anything dealing with software development. It's just a bad idea.*

Changing an asterisk to a different shade of green sounds like a simple change. But unless it's defined exactly what that shade is, why it should be that new shade, and the people asking for it know they will be happy with it, the simple request for changing the shade of green may turn into hours or days of back-and-forth with the developer. Don't laugh, I've seen it happen. My former coworker ended up spending nearly two days going back and forth with a business, changing the size and color shade of a single character on the site. Afterward, he decorated his cube with a large green asterisk drawn with a whiteboard marker on paper and stapled to the wall. It was a testament to inefficiency. If you were told, as the owner of the business, that hundreds or thousands of dollars had been spent to get an asterisk to the right size and shade of green, it would be understandable if you were upset.

And yet, this sort of thing happens all the time.

PDF Combinatorics

In a more recent example, the team was asked to allow a system to build a single large PDF report out of what started as many individual small reports for a large number of medical caregivers. As it stood, the system was capable of generating a calendar "report" of each caregiver's assignments for the month. The request was to allow a user of our software to select a bunch of caregivers and generate all of these individual calendars for use by the coordinators.

We were, and still are, using a reporting software that allows us to build reports. One of the features is that reports can contain sub-reports, potentially ad infinitum. Our developer managed to take in the list of caregivers and combine the individual reports into one, but one particular issue was causing him fits. In certain places in the report and at the end, a blank page was inserted into the final PDF. We gathered several developers and made all sorts of attempts to get rid of these superfluous blank pages, but to no avail. After a few days, we concluded that it was not going to allow us to remove these blank pages. We reported this to the customer.

Their response was rather surprising. It didn't matter to them because they were using this to print out each of the individual calendars and then scan and email them out to the individual caregivers. What?! Finally, we had the real problem that needed a solution—the electronic delivery of the calendars to the caregivers. We could have simply iterated through the selected caregivers, generated each report in turn, and emailed the result to the caregiver. Instead, we were given a potential "solution" but not given enough insight into the problem to determine a better solution.

I know that Agile software development practices are typically either loved or hated, but regardless, the standard story format does have a lot of value. "As a {role or user} I want {feature or change} so I can {benefit}." There's a lot of potential value in a sentence with that format. If the request above was spelled out this way, then it would have been the responsibility of the developers to ask questions that would have led to the right solution.

"As a scheduling coordinator, I want to be able to build combined caregiver schedules so I can print, scan, and email them to the caregivers without contracting arthritis from too many mouse clicks." In this case, the majority of the valuable information in the request is in the "benefit" or supposed benefit. If the goal is to deliver the report to each caregiver, then printing and scanning are not necessary. The amount of effort could have been reduced to selecting a list of caregivers and clicking a button. The system could then have generated and delivered those calendars. Enhancing the solution even further, depending on the selections, most or potentially all of the work could have been automated. If the caregivers are associated with the coordinator and they all need their calendars on a specific schedule, the selection could be made via a database query and the triggering of all of this could be done via a cron job. The scheduling coordinator now has one less thing to worry about and we've delivered a real solution to the real problem instead of an imagined solution to an unexplained and misunderstood concern.

Other misunderstood requirements have led to such erroneous features as load-bearing notes, exceedingly complex data structures that allowed employees, copy machines, meeting rooms, and MRI machines to be treated in exactly the same way. By taking the time to understand exactly what is needed and **why**, we get a better solution, and we'll often get it cheaper and faster as well. Speaking of which…

The Iron Triangle of Software Development

Many of you may be familiar with the so-called "iron triangle" of software development. On each of the sides of this triangle are "Good," "Fast," and "Cheap," or, in other versions, "Quality," "Speed," and "Cost." In any given software project, you're only able to pick up to two of them. If we pick "Good" and "Fast," we're going to need an excellent team, which will not be cheap. If we pick "Good" and "Cheap," we can get something like open-source software: people volunteering what time they can, mostly for free. The resulting software can be very good, but since it's all on volunteer time, we cannot dictate how long before it is done. If the choice is "Fast" and "Cheap," perhaps we've got a skilled team on a tight deadline or a team of motivated beginners. Quality will likely suffer.

When we don't take the time to determine what is really needed and figure out the problem we want to solve, there's a good chance that we will only be picking one (or fewer) of our two possibilities from the iron triangle. There's no need for that.

Why Do We Build Software?

We build software for a number of reasons: to scratch an itch, to learn, to solve a problem, to reduce errors, to automate, to make money, or just for fun. Each of these reasons leads to a different answer about how much effort we need to expend to answer the questions about what to build and why.

If you're building an MVP (minimum viable product) or a prototype, fast and cheap may be the best choices. Once it is determined that the product is viable, then time and/or money may be more readily available. The MVP can be scrapped and a better, higher-quality replacement can be stood up in its place.

If we're building an application that we expect to live for a while, then it makes sense to put more time and effort into gathering the correct requirements, solving the problems, and architecting maintainable solutions.

If we're creating code for fun, then it's up to us to determine how much time and effort we want to spend. At the time I'm writing this, the Advent of Code is running. Each day presents a new challenge which can be solved with code. According to the leaderboard, many of these problems could be completed within a few minutes by a small set of elite developers. If you know your language of choice well, and potentially know an algorithm or already have a library with an implementation, the problems can be solved relatively quickly. If you're not familiar with some technologies, it may take a bit longer.

In one of the problems, you're given a list of a group of people along with a happiness change score for each pair of people. For instance, if Bob sits next to Sue, his happiness may increase by 50 points, but hers drops by 10. The problem wants you to determine the optimal seating of people around a table so that the maximum increase in happiness is achieved. The solution I chose borrowed some permutation code from a previous day and generated all possible permutations of the dinner guest order. Since this was for fun, I decided to stop there. I was able to get the correct answer. However, what I wrote was inefficient.

In a circular seating arrangement, many of the permutations are redundant. If everyone gets up and moves a seat to the left, their happiness doesn't change because they are still sitting next to the same people. If you flip the ordering from clockwise to counter-clockwise, all of the guests are still next to the same people and their happiness is unchanged. However, my solution didn't account for this. This means that with an eight-person table, my code was checking 40,320 possibilities. If it accounted for rotations, only 5,040 possibilities would have remained. Since I was running this code once, and then likely never again, the runtime being 8x over an optimized solution wasn't that big of a deal (though it did bother me a bit). If I had code that did this as a service for customers, or for larger tables, the amount of time needed to update the algorithm to only generate what was needed could mean, on a popular service, I may only need 1/8th of the servers and resources. In that case, it makes sense to optimize.

Make it Work, Make it Right, Make it Fast

Once we've determine what to build and why, our next task is to make it happen. This means our first pass at the code can be messy, inefficient, and, to a certain extent, bad. But we should certainly not stop at this phase. Once it is working, we move to the next step, "make it right." This means we clean up the code, put things right. In my throwaway code above, I stopped after making it work. I got the answer I needed. However, in our day jobs or hobbies, if we want code that will last, we need to continue. Making it work involves understanding the problem at a code level—perhaps reaching the point that you know what libraries are needed, how the inputs fit together, even understanding that if you're dealing with a circular permutation, there are a lot fewer possibilities than a standard permutation.

The "make things right" phase is where refactoring can happen. You can DRY (don't repeat yourself) out your code by moving repeated functionality into functions and methods, renaming variables and functions to be more clear about what's happening, potentially simplifying what's going on since our understanding of the problem has likely increased. We can reorganize to make it easier to maintain. This can include tasks like removing calls to creating objects with new inside our constructors and providing those objects via dependency injection.

After the code is cleaned up, the final step is "make it fast." This means that we need to realize there is a trade-off in nearly everything we do. Sometimes we trade runtime for memory. Other times, we might call out to a custom C-compiled extension in order to speed things up, but perhaps at the expense of ease of maintenance.

Of course, the "make it right" and "make it fast" steps are much easier and less scary if you've written tests in order to make it work. Whether you follow a TDD workflow (which I recommend) or you write the tests afterward, having those tests in place as you refactor will allow you to be confident that you haven't traded in your working solution for a better looking, but broken, solution.

Why Being DRY is Not Always Best

As software developers, we have loads of acronyms to help us remember various principles. There's SOLID (ironically, each letter in SOLID stands for its own acronym), KISS (keep it simple, stupid), KICK (keep it complex, knucklehead), DRY (don't repeat yourself), YAGNI (you ain't gonna need it), GRASP (general responsibility assignment software pattern), DDD (domain-driven development), as well as DRY (don't repeat yourself).

We are often taught that DRY is important. We are told that if two bits of code are the same, they should go in a function. If two bits are nearly the same, put the common bits in a function, abstract out the variable parts to the parameters, lather, rinse, repeat. This means that often in my career I've seen designs and software go sideways when what was initially determined to be two different pieces of code doing the same thing, followed by refactoring that to a function, turns out to be two bits of code doing nearly the same thing but for completely different reasons. In that case, the redundant code is arguably less bad than a single complex solution that must account for a plethora of different running conditions.

"Duplication is far cheaper than the wrong abstraction." - Sandi Metz

In some cases, DRYing out our code can actually be harmful. Just because two bits of code appear to be doing the same thing doesn't mean they are. The quote above is by Sandi Metz, an outstanding speaker and software engineer. I encourage you to find her videos and watch them. She is a Ruby developer, but the talks I've seen apply no matter what language you're working in. I highly recommend watching any of her talks or reading what she has written.

The point here links back to the beginning. De-duplication of code just for the sake of having a lower score on `phpcpd` serves no good purpose. It's better to have identical code in a few places while we strive to understand the real problem and determine the real solution than to DRY out the code to a point where we don't understand what's really happening and modifications become costly and potentially impossible. Strive to make your code as simple as you can, but no simpler.

Conclusion

I encourage you to look into the change requests, issues, tickets, stories, or whatever you may call them, and determine what they are really asking. It's our job as software developers to build solutions to real problems, not just to turn one silly request into code after another. We are being paid to think more than we're being paid to type. This means we need to ask the right questions, dig deeper into understanding what we need to do, and provide real solutions to the real problems our customers have. It's not about changing the asterisk to another shade of green, it's about determining why that needs to happen and what problem is being solved.

Chapter

10

Introduction to Product Management for Developers

Joshua Silver

One of the most valuable and underrated skills a developer can master is the ability to think like a product manager. By learning some basic product management skills, developers can improve the quality of their product, open up new career opportunities, and become more well-rounded software engineers.

When discussing the requisite competencies of a well-rounded software engineer, skills such as communication, testing, or DevOps tend to come up much more frequently than product management. However, after many years of leading an R&D organization, I firmly believe that one of the most valuable and underrated skills a developer can master is the ability to think like a product manager.

For developers who tire of programming on a daily basis, product management is a common career progression that leverages the technical proficiency built as a coder but provides for a very different daily routine. Even for those not looking to give up development, product management is still a great way to expand one's influence, responsibility, and possibly even level of seniority within an organization—all without requiring formal training or years of hands-on experience. Rather, it's all about learning to think differently.

Developers have long been trained to answer the *"How should the product be built?"* question.

Debates on technical stacks, discussion of implementation details, and heated arguments over the most accurate estimate can be frequently heard amongst software teams. While every organization defines the product management role a bit differently, product managers spend their time answering a very different but equally important set of questions:

1. *What product should be built?*
2. *When should it be built?*
3. *For whom should it be built?*
4. *Why should it be built?*

Unlike the *"how question,"* which has starts with a defined deliverable, these two questions are about defining the end goal and tend to be much more broad. Typically, most markets are wide open for innovation and possibilities abound. In the later sections **Defining Feature Scope, Timeline, and Priorities** and **Understanding the "Why,"** I'll explain how to answer these questions by thinking like a product manager, and I'll also share some useful "tricks of the trade" that you can put to immediate use—even during your current development project.

Defining Feature Scope, Timeline, and Priorities

One of the most important skills needed to be successful at product management is the ability to appropriately determine the scope of a given feature. Product managers stand at the intersection of several key teams within a company. Sales and marketing, always wanting to have the "latest and greatest" and not wanting to fall behind the competition, never fail to serve up a long list of feature requests, no matter the scope. Account management and customer service want every last bug fixed—no matter how remote an edge case. Development wants time to refactor code and pay down technical debt. And finally, the executive team, well, they just want the current release to be done yesterday. Product managers must listen to feedback from all of these key stakeholders and make the tough decisions about which features get slated for development and which ones fail to even make it onto the product roadmap or development backlog.

Once the product roadmap is created, features are broken down into smaller chunks of work—usually called user stories or tickets. Even if tickets or user stories are fairly prescriptive, as a developer, there is a usually a lot of latitude regarding implementation details. For example, should a particular setting be hardcoded, added to an application configuration file, or placed into a database? Should the setting be adjustable in code, via a client-facing settings screen, or through an internal-facing administrative console? Each one of these seemingly small decisions has major ramifications on the product. Critical tradeoffs must be made between upfront development effort, ongoing maintenance effort, and customizability on a per-client basis.

As the overall feasibility of a feature and the aforementioned technical tradeoffs are being discussed, software engineers typically fall into one of two camps.

The first is the "Can't Be Done" camp. Developers in the "Can't Be Done" camp never really want to build anything new (despite being developers!) or make major modifications to a legacy system. They actively fight to keep the scope extremely limited and are never short on excuses (e.g., "It doesn't work that way in our system," "It will take too long to build," "You just don't understand how the system operates," etc.) Even the slightest hint of technical complication spirals into a project that "could take forever."

The second camp developers fall into is the "Anything Is Possible" camp. These developers err on the side of action and always want to build something quickly. They thrive on technical complication, genuinely believe that they can "crank it out" in a matter of days or weeks, and have a blatant disregard for the level of effort it will take to maintain their codebase on an ongoing basis.

The reality is that both of these attitudes are outright dangerous. If you subscribe to the "Can't Be Done" philosophy, nothing will ever get done, and innovation will stagnate. On the flip side, by believing that anything is possible and building anything and everything quickly, system stability suffers and technical debt abounds.

So, as a developer, how can you avoid being caught up in the "Anything Is Possible" or "Can't Be Done" schools of thought and start thinking like a product manager to achieve the right balance of scope?

Tricks of the Trade: Defining Feature Scope, Timeline, and Priorities

1. Simplify Everything by 20%

When defining the initial scope of a feature, typically, about 20% of the requested functionality is "nice to have" versus true "need to have," even if the customer suggests otherwise. By focusing on the valuable 80% and forgoing the "wasted" 20%, the timeline and product complexity can be greatly reduced. The hard part, of course, is figuring out which feature is valuable and which is waste, particularly when all of them are inevitably listed as equally important.

The easiest way to make this determination is to demo incremental milestones or interim releases to a group of end users and solicit candid feedback. Users who will have to live with the software on a daily basis can be counted on to be pretty vocal about what's missing.

For those working in a lean or agile environment, remember that the next version doesn't need to be perfect; it only needs to add value and be significantly better than the last version. This is the very definition of iteration.

And for those who use a more traditional waterfall software development lifecycle, when a release is inevitably running late (show me a large release that is not behind!), you can use this technique to determine what should be delivered first, so at least something can be delivered by the deadline.

2. Plan for the Long Term, but Find Early Wins

It usually only takes about five minutes when discussing a new ticket before the conversation turns to the age-old question of how much refactoring needs to be done in order to accommodate the change.

While there is no universal right answer and it's largely dependent upon the specific system in question, a good general goal is to find the proverbial "low-hanging fruit." There is usually at least SOME portion of the ticket that can be delivered easily and quickly without much refactoring. That's generally the best place to start.

The same goes for determining which tasks to work on first in any given sprint or development phase. While many developers gravitate toward either the easiest first (get at least something completed quickly) or the hardest first (get the challenging tasks out of the way so the rest is easy), a much better prioritization method is to deliver whatever will provide the most value to the end user first. I like to call this "value-first" prioritization.

Remaining focused on the business need and end-user value creation is the key way that developers can begin to think more like product managers.

Understanding the "Why"

In many development groups, the modus operandi is to begin coding immediately after receiving a development ticket, without giving much thought as to why the work is even being done in the first place.

I often remind my team that a mediocre developer will do his or her best to complete all requirements after reading through a ticket several times; a good developer will ask the ticket author clarifying questions to really hone in on the requirements so as to not only can meet but wholly exceed expectations. A great developer will strive to inherently understand how customers use the product and won't begin development until he or she fully grasps *WHY* this feature is being built. A great developer will strive to deliver the highest-quality product, even if that means pushing back on customer requests and suggesting changes to the ticket requirements.

By understanding WHY the work is being done, a developer is much more likely to make good tradeoffs during the implementation phase. More importantly, he or she is building a strong sense of customer empathy. Being empathetic to customers is a critical trait of successful product managers, as it helps to ensure that customer needs are at the forefront of any major technical decision.

So how does a developer actually "Understand the Why" and demonstrate customer empathy?

At my company, Patientco, we routinely devote development time so that all of our software engineers can experience "a day in the life" of our customers. During these days, our developers have the opportunity to travel to a customer's office or worksite and observe firsthand how end users actually interact with our product. They are able to gain a better appreciation for the challenges that our users face—while interacting both with our product and with the healthcare industry, in general. More importantly, they increase their intuition (or "Spidey Sense") about what customers will actually like or dislike.

These "day in the life" events have turned out to be a really effective tool and a win-win for our company, our clients, and our development team. It turns out that customers are incredibly appreciative that we take the time to deeply learn about their organization, and they feel a small sense of ownership as they helped educate the product's creators. Equally, developers appreciate the investment we have made in their professional and personal development. Overall, the results have been phenomenal, and we have been able to get some easy wins when developers identified some "low-hanging fruit" and were able to make some small code changes that yielded big results. More importantly, our developers are able to empathize with our customers.

In my experience, having a culture around customer empathy not only improves the feature-functionality balance of the product, but the overall quality of work also increases substantially. Gone are the days of a developer admitting that something didn't feel right when he or she coded it but let it go anyway, only to be caught by QA. You see, when developers have personally met end users and know how much pain any uncaught bugs will cost those users, they tend to spend more time testing their code before submitting it to QA.

Tricks of the Trade: Understanding the "Why"

1. Talk to Customers and Learn Their Usage Patterns

Even if an onsite visit to a customer site is not possible, there are still many other casual ways to for developers to gain a better appreciation for "The Why." Joining account review calls with account management is a great way to learn how current customers are using the product and to hear firsthand any suggestions or complaints about the product. Equally, keeping an eye open for any prospect objections while going on a sales call (either in person or via WebEx) is a quick way to improve one's understanding of how sales departments actually sell the product and what resonates with prospects.

For those who want to really deepen their understanding of customer usage patterns, it's never a bad idea to ask a current customer if the team can watch them (via screenshare or in person) for an hour or two as they go about their daily routine of using the product. In product management parlance, this is called an ethnographic field study because participants are observed in their normal environment. Often, simply watching end users interact with the product for a short period will unearth surprising findings. For example, advanced users may have implemented workarounds to overcome a product bug or feature deficiency or something that was assumed to be obvious but was anything but intuitive!

2. Remember that Actions Speak Louder than Words

When thinking like a product manager, it is vitally important to spend time interacting with, observing, and talking to customers to understand why they are doing a particular action or, in some cases, why they are NOT doing what was expected. However, short direct observations, anecdotes from customer service, and self-reported responses (e.g. responding to a survey) don't always tell the full story. Therefore, it is always a good idea to compliment these qualitative points with quantitative ones.

Furthermore, if you are working on a consumer product (where users span a wide range of personas) or you don't have the opportunity to directly interact with customers, data can often be used as a good proxy for user behavior. With the proliferation of analytics tools (many of which are free), there is no longer any excuse for not knowing, in detail, how customers are using the product.

It's not all that uncommon for users to report that they are doing one thing but to have backend analytics show a very different usage pattern. For example, imagine that a customer insists he or she needs another option added to a dropdown menu, which already has ten options. The "Anything Is Possible" developer probably would have just added the option to the menu and moved on to the next ticket. Meanwhile, the "Can't Be Done" developer is likely still debating the technical complexity of adding this extra option and brainstorming reasons for why it can't be done.

However, the developer who is thinking like a product manager is not worried about the technical complexity but rather is worried that the menu is actually already too long and that adding another option would just make the product even less usable. That developer pulls some quick data on how frequently each of the existing options is actually used, and it turns out that only two of the ten options are used in 95% of user selections. By weighing the raw usage data with the customer feature request, a good solution can be created, which removes a lot of the unused options and repurposes one of the lesser-used options to accomplish exactly what the customer needs. This is another win-win situation, as the customer got what he or she wanted, the developer spent less time coding, and all users benefited from a simpler product.

Recommended Reading

If you are seriously considering a career transition from software development to product management, invest some time reading one of the many books, websites, and blogs dedicated to the subject, some recommendations are below.

- *The Lean Startup*, by Eric Reis
- *The Hard Thing About Hard Things: Building a Business When There Are No Easy Answers Hardcover*, by Ben Horowitz
- *Getting Real: The Smarter, Faster, Easier Way to Build a Successful Web Application*, by Jason Fried
- *The Four Steps to the Epiphany*, by Steve Blank
- *The Design of Everyday Things*, by Donald A. Norman
- *Lean Software Development: An Agile Toolkit*, by Mary Poppendieck and Tom Poppendieck

Next Steps

Even if you plan to stay coding full time, as you embark on your next project, take some time to think like a product manager and put your new skills to work using these four "tricks of the trade." Your users will love the fact that product quality has been improved and that the features that directly meet their needs are being delivered faster than ever.

Chapter 11

Choose Your Own Adventure— Freelancer or Founder?

Joshua Warren

You know you like working for yourself, and could not imagine working an office job ever again. More opportunities are opening up for you as a freelance developer and at some point you have to decide if you are a freelancer or a founder. As a freelancer-turned-founder, I've been there. In this article, I'll talk about the pros and cons of being a freelancer versus building a company. I will then explain what you need to know when you make this decision, and how to execute either choice.

Starting Out

Freelance developers often find themselves the victim of their own success. As a freelancer, there are only two ways to grow your business beyond a certain point. First, you can raise the hourly rate you charge—an option many developers aren't comfortable with and that has an upper limit. The other option is to spend more and more of your waking hours working for your clients. This option can serve as a temporary boost to your business. However, the long-term impact on your health, relationships, and well being make this a poor choice.

As a freelance developer you will reach a point where you have to make a choice. You can continue to work as a solo freelancer, or you can grow your business into a development agency. Many freelancers look at agency owners and feel they have it made. Many agency owners long for a return to their freelancing days. It's not a simple choice—it's a complicated decision.

The Pros and Cons of Freelancing

As a lone freelancer, you are your business. Your planning and decision making can focus completely on yourself. As long as the work is getting done, you can work when you want, where you want, how you want. Your expenses are much lower than they would be for an agency. You are able to be much more agile—following new technologies and ideas faster than most agencies could dream of. You're able to spend your time focused on the things that you find most interesting. You don't have to deal with the overhead and administration that comes with an agency or any other desk job.

Life as a freelance developer, however, has its drawbacks. While technology allows us to work from anywhere in the world, we still have to stay plugged in. The thought of taking a completely unplugged vacation of more than a few days is a dream for most freelance developers.

Working as a freelance developer can be risky. Your entire income comes from the work you do, so if you are unable to work, you are unable to earn income.

Finally, there are social and personal development drawbacks to working as a freelance developer. Coworking and Twitter mean that freelance developers can tie themselves into a larger community. However, as a freelance developer you don't find yourself working with the same people on projects. You work individually and miss the feedback and camaraderie you get from working with the same team of developers.

The Pros and Cons of Owning a Development Agency

Some freelance developers view building a development agency as the golden ticket. To them, it seems to be a way to work less, get rich, and retire early. Unfortunately, it's not that easy! There are certainly benefits to owning a development agency. You are no longer limited by the number of waking hours in the day. By growing a team of talented developers to work alongside you, you multiply the hours of work you can complete for your clients. In turn, you are able to generate a greater amount of revenue.

By building a development agency you can surround yourself with great developers. This allows you to have the experience of working with the same team on projects, helping you to improve your skills.

There are also drawbacks to building and owning a development agency. While your revenue is higher, your costs are higher as well. Besides costs being higher, your costs are more fixed. As a freelance developer, you have the flexibility to alter your spending somewhat as revenue climbs or falls. Once you have employees, an office, and other recurring expenses, there is more pressure to meet a certain level of revenue consistently.

That's not the only pressure, either. As the owner of a development agency, your employees depend on you to grow and operate the business to ensure they receive a paycheck. Imagine the pressure as a freelance developer to earn enough money to support your own needs multiplied by ten—once for each employee.

You also will find yourself with less time to spend on actual development. The good news is that as your agency grows, the time you do spend on development can be on topics you choose because they are interesting to you. The bad news is that this time can be challenging to find. You have to delegate even the interesting development work to your team, or your agency will never be successful.

While more agencies consist of distributed teams, the average agency does maintain an office. It can be challenging to work remotely or travel, especially in the early days of building a development agency.

How to Choose

Life as a freelance developer or as the owner of a development agency isn't perfect. So, how do you choose which of these options is right for you? There's no magic answer that works for everyone, but there is a way to find the right option for you. It breaks down to five steps:

1. Determine your goals, and the goals of your family.

2. Check if your freelance career can meet those goals.

3. Check if building a development agency can meet those goals.

4. Determine whether you can build a development agency.

5. Build a business plan for your development agency.

Determine Your Goals

The first, and most important, step is to determine your goals and the goals of your family. Where do you want to be in 5 years? 10 years? First you should determine the lifestyle you would like and the amount of income you will need for that lifestyle. More importantly, you should also consider the less tangible benefits of freelancing. Develop a budget for not just money but also your time. How much time do you want to spend working from an office? How much time do you want to spend working from home? How much time do you want to spend not working?

Also, what aspects of your work do you enjoy, and what aspects do you dislike? Is never having to worry about sales, marketing, or contracts attractive to you? Do you enjoy being involved in every aspect of interacting with your clients?

Check if Your Freelance Career Can Meet Those Goals

Take a look at the budgets for both time and money you built in the previous step, along with your goals. Is it possible for you to meet those numbers and goals as a freelancer? For instance, if you want to work 40 hours a week, take 2 weeks off a year, and make $250,000 a year, that works out to billing $125/hour. Based on your experience as a freelancer and the most successful freelancers in your field, is that realistic? If it's not, it's time to determine whether you can meet those goals by building a development agency. If it does, and if you are more excited about the idea of working as a freelancer than building a development agency—great! You're one of the lucky ones who can find fulfillment in a long-term freelance career, so keep doing what you're doing. In this case, turn to the section Building a Freelance Career for your next steps.

Check if Building a Development Agency Can Meet Those Goals

Take those goals you evaluated in the previous step and compare them against the idea of building a development agency. For instance, if one of your goals is to always be able to work by yourself, building a development agency isn't a good option for you.

Figure 1: The first two Creatuity employees, in Poznan

It's possible that after measuring your goals against these options you find you can't reach them via either method. That's a sign that you should stop, go back to the first step, and think through the goals and budget you've set to make sure they are realistic.

Determine If You Can Build a Development Agency

You've determined your freelance career can't meet your goals, but building an agency can. Your next step is to determine whether you can build a development agency. What is your experience, training, and comfort level in business, money management, human resources, and sales? It's normal to have areas where you feel less qualified or that you enjoy less. But if any of these are areas that for some reason you absolutely cannot work in, you will have a hard time building a development agency.

Build a Business Plan for Your Development Agency

It doesn't matter if you never show it to a single person; before you get started, build a business plan for your development agency. If you can't finish the business plan, most likely you won't be able to finish the work that goes into starting and growing an agency. The process of building this plan will also help you check to see if your agency will meet your goals. This plan also gives you a timeframe to share with your family before starting on this journey. Only once you've built this plan and shared this timeline should you start to build your development agency. Once you're ready to start, turn to the section Building a Development Agency to receive your next steps.

Building a Freelance Career

You have found that continuing as a freelance developer will allow you to meet your goals—that's great news!

Knowing that you can meet your goals isn't where you should stop. Your next step is to make sure that you continue to grow and build a true freelancing career. This will keep you on track to meeting those goals as soon as possible.

The first step to take to build your freelancing career is to become more involved in the development community. This could be the community surrounding the programming language you prefer. It could also be the community for the application your work involves. Find this community and connect with them. For some communities this might be best done via Twitter, others on IRC, GitHub, StackExchange, or even Reddit. As you become more involved in the community you should attend conferences and other community events as much as you can.

This community involvement is important to a freelancer for a few reasons. First, it replaces the social and technical interaction you would receive with a team if you built or worked at an agency. By engaging with the community you can sharpen your skills and stay up to date on the technology you use. At the same time, you will get to know others doing the same work as you.

Both successful freelancers and agencies often receive more requests than they are able to meet. Sometimes a client prefers to work with an individual or wants to work with someone in a specific city. In those cases, developers and agencies have to turn down clients and refer them to others. By becoming more involved in your community, you can receive those referrals. As you build your freelancing career you might become one of the people referring potential clients to other freelancers. By being involved with the community you can know that those referrals will be handled well.

The most important thing you can do at this point is to write down those goals you set, and stick to them. If your goal is to reach $250,000 in income and you reach it—great! Celebrate your success and find ways to tailor your freelancing career to ensure that you maintain this level. Too often freelancers reach their goals, only to decide to set their goals even higher. There's nothing wrong with challenging yourself. But if you push yourself to increase your income higher and higher, your personal well-being and the quality of your work will suffer. The most successful, happiest freelancers are those who know how much money they need to make and how much time they want to spend making that money. They have the self-control that when they hit those numbers, they stop. Build your freelancing career towards reaching your goals—not only your income goal, but also your goals for how you spend your time.

Building a Development Agency

So you're ready to start on the adventure of building a development agency. Great! You have your business plan in hand, and are ready to turn your successful freelancing experience into an agency. Let's get started.

Learn What You Don't Know

When you first start out, you will be filling many roles in your agency that will eventually be filled by trained professionals. It's important to determine what these roles are, and admit to yourself what you don't know. Knowing what you don't know and what you don't like doing will give you a roadmap for what you need to learn and who your first hires should be.

Plan Ahead

Moving from working as a freelance developer to building a development agency is challenging. One of the best things you can do is to be aware of some of the challenges and plan for them. For instance, as you grow your development agency, you will most likely have to raise your rates. Agencies have larger teams, more specialists, and in turn higher costs. You also will find yourself facing times when you have to rely on your team to interact with your clients. At times, you won't have enough time in the day to both maintain and grow your agency and interact with clients. Both of these changes can be jarring to clients that have been with you since you were a freelance developer, so it's important to plan for those times. At some point, you will have to refer those clients to other freelancers who might be a better fit for their needs. If you don't, you will find yourself and your new agency struggling to meet the needs of those former freelance clients and your new clients. Planning for that transition can guide your interactions with your freelancing clients as you begin to build your development agency.

Build a Team

Your main hiring focus should be developers. Depending on the technology you work with, it may be challenging to find qualified, skilled developers. Keep an eye out for these developers and each time an opportunity arises, add them to your team.

However, a successful development agency needs more than just developers to survive and thrive. Go back to your goals as well as the list of items you don't like, or don't know. Use that to map out the kind of help you need. Many excellent developers do a good job at managing tasks and projects but discover they are terrible at things like marketing. That's fine—it shows you that your team should include someone who can handle any marketing needed for your growing development agency.

Know your own personality, and tailor your initial hires around it. For instance, if you are creative but tend to be less organized, your early hires should be people who are organized and can help keep things organized.

Bootstrapping

Development agencies aren't built on venture capital. They are built on the hard work, dedication, and oftentimes the savings of their founders. Development agencies, however, are easier to bootstrap than many other businesses. Especially when you're first starting out, you don't need to spend a lot of money buying assets and equipment. So, many freelance developers use the money they receive from a large project to invest in the development agency they're founding. That money can be used to start the business and your initial hires can be other freelance developers who only work when you have work for them. This allows you to build a lean company that can be grown from the revenue received from each project. This lack of assets and lean approach,

Figure 2: The Poznan team with the author in October 2012

however, means that many new development agencies have little cash in reserve. During this time of your agency's growth, it's important to be financially conservative. It's better to grow slowly and steadily and continue to bootstrap your agency than to bet it all on one big contract.

Make it Awesome

Building a development agency gives you a unique opportunity. Many of us become freelance developers because we don't enjoy working for the average company. So, don't build an average company. Don't build a company that requires its developers to work in all those ways you don't like. Build something unique, something awesome. Build a company and an office where developers love to work. This goes beyond perks and to the core of your company. As you build your policies and structure your company, don't think just about getting the job done. Think about how you can create a positive experience for your developers and other team members as well as your clients.

In his book Delivering Happiness, Tony Hsieh relates the story of building a successful multi-million dollar company. At some point, Tony realizes that he hates going to work every day at the company that he had built. Don't make that mistake. Throughout the early days of your development agency, focus on building a company that you enjoy working for. It's better to make slow progress towards your goals and to build a positive company that you and your employees enjoy working for than to reach your goals quickly but find yourself despising the path you took to get there.

Now What?

So you're ready to start building your development agency. You have an idea of your strengths and weaknesses, you are planning ahead, and you're ready to start building your team. However, you might realize that there's more to starting a company and building it into a successful development agency than this. And you're right—everything that it takes to get an agency off the ground could fill a book!

So for now, take these basics and get started, but realize there's still more for you to learn. One of the most challenging, but most rewarding, aspects of building a development agency is that you will be constantly learning new things. Take advantage of this opportunity, and when in doubt, reach out to the community. Reach out not only to the development community, but also the community of developers-turned-founders. There's few of us, but we're out here, ready to help and encourage you on your journey from developer to founder.

Chapter 12

On the Value of a Degree...

Eli White

Recently I got into a discussion with a good friend who was considering going back to school after having over a decade of experience in her industry. Many other people were chiming in, saying how going back to school late in their career was the best choice they ever made and how it opened up so many doors for them.

Now not everyone in that conversation was a computer programmer, but it brought this topic back to mind for me about our industry at least.

Initial Value and Types of Degrees

If you knew me 10–15 years ago, when I was working for startups and involved in many hiring decisions, I was vehement that it was important for everyone to have a degree in Computer Science. The grounding in theory that Computer Science gives you helps guide good coding practices. Many issues that I saw in software design could be linked back to simply not understanding some of the core logic, algorithms, and theories of Computer Science in the first place.

At the time, I dismissed people who had degrees in related fields, such as Computer Engineering or Information Systems. When I got involved in hiring at Digg.com, I was often frustrated when the management would engage many younger recent high-school graduates who had no formal training in Computer Science. However, in these cases, it was not just that they did not have *the degree,* it was also that they had little to no experience.

> *The only source of knowledge is experience.*
>
> — *Albert Einstein*

The Value of Experience

You see, one thing that I firmly believe in at this point is that experience is truly what matters. Say, someone has a recent B.S. in C.S. and no experience and someone else does not have a degree but does have ten years of experience. I would take the experienced person in a heartbeat. (This assumes, of course, that the good experience comes with good referrals.)

The value of experience just cannot be underrated. Every year that you spend writing production code, fixing bugs, and dealing with "real world" problems outweighs whether you can calculate the Big O notation of a function.

More importantly to my friend's situation, in the modern workforce every hiring manager worth his or her salt will understand this. If you have ten years of experience, unless you are specifically looking for a government job that (incorrectly) *requires* a certain degree, going back for your degree does not gain you anything.

Essentially, getting a degree is a way to get the "equivalent of experience" when you do not have any expertise in that field yet. Once you have the experience, you do not need the degree. The feeling that many people in that conversation were having amounted to a variation of Imposter Syndrome. They assumed they could not get the job they wanted without having the degree but never applied for the position to find out.

None of this, of course, applies if you are looking to switch fields because you are entering a new field without any experience.

The Current (and Future) Generations

My son has just entered sixth grade and has started thinking a bit about what he wants to do when he grows up. Currently, I am getting to play the role of proud father, especially when he keeps saying that he wants to "help do PHP" with me.

So what advice will I give him in six years when he is graduating from high school? Assuming he still wants to be a programmer, I would still suggest that he go to school and get a solid grounding in Computer Science. I feel that for someone starting fresh out of the gate, it is an excellent way to get knowledge under your belt and is probably worth about three years worth of experience.

Moreover, it is much easier to get the degree and then a job than to attempt to get a job immediately out of high school and find those three years of experience in the early days. However, hey, if you find yourself in a situation where the job can be found, and you take some training courses toward that—once again, experience is really where the deepest value exists.

Chapter 13

Resume 101

Jordan Tway

The business side of being a developer is what to know, who to connect with, and how to sell yourself. As a technical recruiter, I have conversations with analysts, managers, and developers every day. Some are currently employed or looking for a new step in their career while others are unemployed, looking to get back to work. In addition to the job seekers, I connect with multiple companies on a daily basis that are looking to hire IT professionals for contract, contract-to-hire, and direct hire positions. Each company has their own specifics, requirements, and needs in each open position. This article will attempt to help sum up the most important factors of what employers and recruiters look for in a resume, an interview, and an overall candidate.

Job searching starts with a well-designed and executed resume. That may seem like a simple task to complete, but resumes come in many shapes, formats, and sizes and unfortunately, many with their fair share of spelling errors. A resume should be simple, straight to the point, and easy to read as it is the most important tool in the job search. In today's marketplace, a resume can also include a LinkedIn account, online portfolio, and personalized website. The less clutter of words and paragraphs that a hiring manager has to read through, the better. Robert Half International has completed studies that conclude it takes an employer approximately 15 seconds to base a decision on a resume. That is not much time to make an impression! The structure of a resume varies, but key aspects should include:

- Object Summary: Include a brief background sentence, your most relatable strengths for the position, and your objectives for career growth.
- Technical Skills: This can include classes taken, and any programming/database languages used in a freelance or professional setting.
- Professional Experience: Be sure to have this section in chronological order and use bullet points for each position.
- Education: Any sort of classes taken, degrees completed, or certifications held.

Personally, I find thhe order shown in the list above to be the easiest to read and the easiest to follow when reviewing candidates for potential jobs. Pretty basic stuff so far, right? Additional information that boosts a resume and illustrates skills even further can include:

- an online portfolio
- a personal website
- a company's website URL

Additionally, if possible or legal, it is always a plus when you can include links to websites to show examples of your previous work.

Next, be sure to double-check your spelling because spelling errors are likely the number one killer of resumes! It may seem like a simple or obvious point, but employers often take candidates completely out of consideration for a spelling error on their resume. Be sure to use spell check and have a peer review your resume before submitting it for any sort of application!

A resume may seem like a simple thing to complete, but it is a very important tool in your job search. Be sure to take the time it deserves so that it illustrates your strengths as best as possible.

Once you have your resume formatted and everything has been spelled correctly, let's say that it has succeeded in landing you a couple of interviews for new positions. In reality, the hard part of getting through the application process is over. Now it is time to ask the right questions, sell your skills, and illustrate how hiring you is a good career move and will benefit the company. Before going into any interview, whether it is with Human Resources or the direct manager, learn about the company. Research the company history, read their blogs or blogs about them, learn about the industry they serve as well as why they are successful as a company. Another highly beneficial tip in preparing for an interview is doing research on the people who will be holding the interview. Knowing where they came from and their background will help you make a connection with them. LinkedIn is a great tool for this! Additional interview tips include:

- Dress professionally, no matter what company it is. It is always possible to dress down for future interviews but you can only make a first impression once.

- Greet the interviewers with a firm handshake. This starts the interview off well and shows you are confident and ready to go!
- Make eye contact. Stay engaged with the individual talking.
- Have a few examples of ROI (Return On Investment - things that saved or earned the company money) that you may have helped with in a previous job or project. The bottom line is the company will hire you to improve their business.
- Before the interview, make a list of questions to ask in regards to the position. Throughout the interview, those questions might be answered, but it will help to have a list in case they are not.
- If you were let go from your previous position, be prepared - with references and examples - to explain why you are still a great candidate for future positions.

Follow the interview up with a thank you email, phone call, or better yet, a hand-written note. Thank the people for their time and consideration during the interview. There is a lot more planning and time that goes into an interview than you may realize. Imagine trying to set aside an hour of your day to interview a potential new employee and still get all of your regular duties accomplished. Then multiply that effort by multiple candidates. It is not easy!

Interviewing can be quite stressful, but the more preparation and confidence you have gathered, the better it will go. Along with doing research and being prepared, having questions to ask during the interview is a good thing as well. To compliment pre-interview preparation, listed below are basic but important questions to ask at the beginning or the end of an interview. Not only does asking questions clear things up for you, it also shows the person interviewing that you are interested in the company and the position. Good questions include:

- **Why is the position open?** Knowing this may give you some insight into why former employees have left or on the flip side, let's you know that the company is growing and expanding their department.
- **What are the growth opportunities in the next 3-5 years?** Everyone wants to grow and advance their career. Having growth opportunities and upward mobility is important, especially in the ever-changing IT field.
- **What are the technology advancements within the company in the next 3-5 years?** This is a commonly-asked question that I receive. It is important to find a company that will stay up with the current market trends in technology. This is especially important if upward mobility is important to you.
- **Who will I be reporting to? A technical lead or a non-technical lead?** Having a good rapport with a direct manager is important for job satisfaction. This is also essential for team dynamics and how a company operates. Reporting to a non-technical individual may present problems in the development environment.
- **What is the team structure?**
- **What development methodology is used?**

- **What initiatives are in place to ensure the technology and frameworks being used don't becomes stagnant or outdated?** This question is especially important if you are the kind of person who likes to keep things current.
- **Does this position offer remote work or a flexible schedule?**
- **What are the pay and vacation time?** This should, preferably, not be the first questions asked. Pay, benefits, and vacation time are very important in a position, but be careful with this question. Asking too soon can paint the picture that the work and the company are not important to you. That will not make a good impression.

This list of questions can help to determine if the position is a good fit for you or if you should keep on searching. Like I mentioned previously, asking questions is a positive sign that you are showing interest. By asking the right questions and doing research on the company, position, and managers, you can look and feel confident interviewing for the position!

Things I Look For in a Candidate When Recruiting

As I mentioned previously, I am a recruiter for Robert Half Technology in Madison, Wisconsin. Robert Half Technology is a leading technology staffing provider for IT professionals and companies all over the world. As a recruiter, I work with IT professionals that are looking for contract, contract-to-hire, or direct hire positions in the Madison market place. Working with multiple openings and multiple candidates at the same time can be quite challenging, but I thrive on this challenge! Obviously, every person and situation is different, but below are key things that I look for when working with people. This list contains my personal preferences, but is likely typical for any other recruiters. The following are the key aspects I look for.

Strong Technical Skills

This can be an objective topic, but examples of work help to prove what you know. Often technical evaluations can be a huge marketing tool for candidates as well. Technical evaluations can be given through the staffing company or from the specific company. These can help hiring professionals get over questions they have on the resume by showing proof of skills. Also, an online portfolio is very helpful for more front-end or design-based positions.

Solid Resume and Work History

Having a finely tuned resume before meeting with a recruiter or hiring professional only speeds up the interview process. With a lot of IT positions, speed to market is essential! Do not forget, writing a solid resume, as covered previously in this article, is critical!

Limited Job Hopping and Large Gaps in Work

This applies to contract-to-hire and direct-hire positions more than to contract work, but most employers look for a consistent work history. Short stints with companies or a large employment gap can raise red flags with employers very quickly and may hurt the chances of earning an interview. If there are large gaps or short stints, be sure to have valid reasoning for them and references from those positions. Technical skills and capabilities can trump work gaps.

Diverse Development Background

Clients want the most well-rounded person they can get. Experience working on web applications, desktop applications, and both back-end and front-end development is great for the next job. The more the tools in the tool bag, the more attractive you are to employers and the more money you can earn.

Quick Response

I look for quick responses from people I work with because in today's market place, things move very quickly! Going from completed interviews to picking a start date can be a matter of days or even hours. The turnaround time from initial contact to interview to possible offer often is less than a week when working with a staffing company. Not being responsive via phone and email to potential job opportunities and interviews can be detrimental to the position.

Feedback on Interviews

Giving feedback on the interview, like what you viewed as the pros and cons of the interview, is very helpful to the person giving the interview, especially if you are working with a placement agency or recruiter. When working with a recruiter, you can be brutally honest about the interview and the company that is hiring. That feedback will help the recruiter for that particular position who can then find better matches down the road.

Honesty

If you are working with multiple staffing companies at once or have interviews set up on your own, be up front about this. There is often competition between staffing companies, but a lot of times, staffing companies have great relationships with different clients. Leveraging those connections can only help and open up more possibilities!

Realistic Expectations

Having realistic expectations in a job search is very important as well. Wanting too much money or being too picky on the type of development you want can turn off companies and limit the opportunities available to you. There are multiple online resources that list salary ranges in various market places and regions. Do some research about what the market rate for a given salary is before requesting a specific salary amount. Also, doing research on other developers and the company itself can help with expectations of the type of work you will be doing.

These eight characteristics are what I look for in a candidate that I work with on positions. Recruiters are paid to help find people jobs, the more information and conversation between them, the better! Hopefully, these will help you not only when you are working with recruiters, but also for applications that go through HR (Human Resources) individuals as well.

The business side of IT and developer jobs can be foreign to some and a reminder for others.

Overall, I hope this article has been able to give you some helpful hints for drafting up a resume, doing interview preparation, asking the right questions, and working alongside a recruiter or HR individual. By putting all of these aspects together, the process of growing as a professional should be a little bit easier. Please feel free to check out Robert Half Technologies[1] for other market trends, interview help, and a salary guide to research market rates for compensation.

[1] Robert Half Techology - *http://www.rht.com*

Chapter

14

Finding Your Voice

Ole Michaelis

It's (mostly) always the same story: I'm trying to convince some of my friends to finally submit a talk to a conference Call for Papers (CfP), and the answer is always: *"Yeah, I would love to…but I have no idea what I should talk about."* It's time to get over your reservations and find your voice.

Step 1: Finding Your Topic

Since I have been hearing this so often, I want to share some of my thoughts on finding a topic and becoming the best speaker to present on it at any conference.

I started speaking at conferences almost two years ago. Since then, I've been to a lot of conferences. I was very lucky because my CTO back then was an experienced speaker already. He gave me a bunch of good advice and helped me to find my very first topic. Today, I am going to pass this advice on to you.

Share the Story of What You Are Doing

I assume you are getting your monthly paycheck for a reason, which means you are actually adding value to your company's goals. Are you programming new features? Great - go talk about that. How about sharing: 'How we evaluate which features are worth being implemented'? Are you fixing a lot of bugs? That is also a great topic to talk about. How about: 'The top five ways to drill down and find EVERY bug'? You may even be doing a bunch of other stuff besides programming - proper project management, prototyping, or technical evaluations - and these are also great things to talk about.

This brings me to my next point.

Share the Story You Are Absolutely Passionate About

Very often after giving a talk, what I hear is that I'm so passionate about the things I'm talking about. The reason for this is dead simple. I **am** enthusiastic about the things I'm talking about. You should be too. Don't just pick a topic that's worth sharing. Pick a topic where you really feel like it's an amazing thing - it's the one tool, best practice, or workflow that you can't live without anymore!

That being said, there is one last thing you really should know about finding talk topics:

Even Though You Know It, Not Everyone Else Knows It

That's really the biggest takeaway of this whole article. To be able to talk about a topic, you should really feel comfortable with it - whatever it might be. We all know that it usually takes at least a couple of months - or even longer, possibly a year - to dig into something well enough to feel comfortable with it. Which brings us to the actual problem: As soon as you know a topic well enough to be able to speak about it, you feel like the topic is so easy that you expect everyone to already know about it.

YOU ARE WRONG! You should feel special for knowing that thing. Ask your peers if they would be curious to see a talk about that topic.

Step 2: The Abstract

Now that you have a rough idea for a topic, it is time to write a nifty abstract for your idea. Let me tell you my little secret about abstracts: Be as specific as you have to, but try to be as vague as you can get away with. I usually write my abstract without knowing how my story will look in the end. By keeping it a bit vague, you are preserving the chance to change bigger and smaller details while crafting the talk.

If you'd like to get an idea of how other speakers are writing their abstracts, there is a pretty obvious way that most people forget about. When you are reading through a conference program, you are just reading a collection of abstracts (and ones that were successful at that). I only know of a very few number of conferences where they ask speakers to write an extra paragraph, separate from their proposal, for the program. So just read through a bunch of programs from your favorite conferences. This way, you can get an idea of what the best writing style would be.

You are almost there, but there is one last thing to do.

Step 3: Name the Talk!

As we all know, there are just a handful of unsolved problems in Computer Science, and besides printing and dual screen solutions, it's naming things. This, unfortunately, also applies to finding a name for your conference talk. At this step, it's a lot about your creativity. Try to make the audience curious, but don't make false promises. Try to tell them what they can expect and what kind of level your talk will be at…and pack all this information into about 40 to 60 characters. Good luck!

You're Done

I hope this made the process of how to get your paper into a CfP a bit more clear and also encourages you to share what you already know. People speaking at conferences aren't super heroes or super brains. The only difference is that they have realized that they have something to share, and now, you have too!

Related URIs:

- speaking.io by awesome Zach Holman - *http://speaking.io*
- @callbackwomen - *https://twitter.com/CallbackWomen*
- JoindIn's List of Open CfPs - *http://joind.in/event/callforpapers*
- Calling All Papers - *http://callingallpapers.com*

Permissions

- *Professional Development for Professional Developers?* by Steve Grunwell. © Steve Grunwell 2015. Originally published in *php[architect] magazine*, September 2015.
- *Introduction to Product Management for Developers* by Joshua Silver. © Joshua Silver 2015. Originally published in *php[architect] magazine*, August 2015.
- *finally{}: On the Value of a Degree…* by Eli White. ©Eli White 2016. Originally published in *php[architect] magazine*, October 2016.
- *Choose Your Own Adventure—Freelancer or Founder?* by Joshua Warren. © Joshua Warren 2015. Originally published in *php[architect] magazine*, January 2015.
- *More Than Just an "OK" Dev* by Gabriel Somoza. © Gabriel Somoza 2016. Originally published in *php[architect] magazine*, August 2016.
- *Finding Your Voice* by Ole Michaelis. © Ole Michaelis 2014. Originally published in *php[architect] magazine*, March 2014.
- *Leveling Up: How to Burn the Candle at Both Ends* by David Stockton. © David Stockton 2015. Originally published in *php[architect] magazine*, July 2015.
- *Leveling Up: You Had One Job* by David Stockton. © David Stockton 2016. Originally published in *php[architect] magazine*, May 2016.
- *Community Corner: Getting the Most out of a Conference* by Cal Evans. © Cal Evans 2016. Originally published in *php[architect] magazine*, November 2016.
- *PHP Conference Newbies 101* by Trip Witt. © Trip Witt 2015. Originally published in *php[architect] magazine*, April 2015.
- *Community Corner: April 2015* by Joe Devon. © Joe Devon 2015. Originally published in *php[architect] magazine*, April 2015.
- *Two Years of PHPAmersfoort: Running a Local Usergroup* by Stefan Koopmanschap. © Stefan Koopmanschap 2015. Originally published in *php[architect] magazine*, November 2015.
- *Leveling Up: Finding the Solution to the Problem* by David Stockton. © David Stockton 2016. Originally published in *php[architect] magazine*, January 2016.

Index

A

abstraction, 64
agile
  environment, 67
  software development
practices, 61
anxiety, 2, 4, 39, 43–46
architect, 27, 31, 46–47
attendees
  first-time, 38
  professional conference, 33
  recruiting, 55

B

boss, 6, 12, 34, 36, 42, 54
budget, 3, 73–75
bugs, 5, 11, 23, 27, 43, 88
  fixing, 80
  good reporting, 5
  last, 66
  new, 59
  tracker, 19
  uncaught, 69
burnout, 3–4, 19, 21–23, 31
  syndrome, 23
bus factor, 31
business plan, 73, 75–76

C

callbackwomen, 89
Call for Papers (CfP), 39,
87, 89
callingallpapers.com, 89
career
  growth, 82
  path, 29

transition, 70
caregivers, 61
clients, 53, 69, 72–73, 75–76,
78, 85
  freelance, 76
code
  designing, 11
  production, 80
  public, 11, 13
  refactor, 66
  review, 14
  standards, 14
code analysis, static, 15
Code Katas, 5
CodeSniffer, 15
coding standards and best
practices, 14
community
  involvement, 75
  resources, 4
  technical, 10
compensation, 56, 86
Computer Engineering, 79
Computer Science, 31,
79–80, 89
conferences, 2–3, 10, 32–34,
36, 38–42, 47, 50, 52, 56, 75,
87–89
  attending, 41
  organizers, 38–39, 52
  PHP, 33, 37–38, 40
contracts, 73, 81, 84
contract-to-hire, 81, 84
contract work, 84
culture, 18–20, 23, 69

D

death marches, 19, 31
degree, 22, 31, 79–80, 82
dependency injection, 63
depression, 4, 22–23
developer
  community, 38
  core, 46–47
  full-stack, 13
  full-stack integrator, 13–14
  good, 11, 68
  jobs, 85
  junior, 6, 27, 30
  open source web application, 42
  senior level, 32
developers, senior, 25–26,
29–30, 32
development agency, 72–78,
83
development methodology,
83
development team, 13, 18, 69

E

education, 40–41, 82
employers, 3–4, 29, 81–82,
84–85
estimates, 18, 66
evaluations, technical, 84, 88
Evernote, 4

F

Facebook, 40, 47
family, 3, 22, 44, 73, 75
fear, 2, 43–46

php[architect] Books

The php[architect] series of books cover topics relevant to modern PHP programming. We offer our books in both print and digital formats. Print copy price includes free shipping to the US. Books sold digitally are available to you DRM-free in PDF, ePub, or Mobi formats for viewing on any device that supports these.

To view the complete selection of books and order a copy of your own, please visit: *http://phparch.com/books/*.

- **Functional Programing in PHP, 2nd Edition**
  By: Simon Holywell
  ISBN: 978-1940111469

- **Web Security 2016**
  Edited by Oscar Merida
  ISBN: 978-1940111414

- **Docker for Developers**
  By Chris Tankersley
  ISBN: 978-1940111360 (Print edition)

- **Building Exceptional Sites with WordPress & Thesis**
  By Peter MacIntyre
  ISBN: 978-1940111315

- **Integrating Web Services with OAuth and PHP**
  By Matthew Frost
  ISBN: 978-1940111261

- **Zend Framework 1 to 2 Migration Guide**
  By Bart McLeod
  ISBN: 978-1940111216

- **XML Parsing with PHP**
  By John M. Stokes
  ISBN: 978-1940111162

- **Zend PHP 5 Certification Study Guide, Third Edition**
  By Davey Shafik with Ben Ramsey
  ISBN: 978-1940111100

- **Mastering the SPL Library**
  By Joshua Thijssen
  ISBN: 978-1940111001

www.ingramcontent.com/pod-product-compliance
Lightning Source LLC
LaVergne TN
LVHW080101070326
832902LV00014B/2363